COMMON ERRORS IN ENGLISH

GOODWILL'S

COMMON ERRORS IN ENGLISH

MICHAEL BRAGANZA

GOODWILL PUBLISHING HOUSE
B-9, Rattan Jyoti, 18 Rajendra Place
New Delhi - 110 008 (INDIA)

Published by :
GOODWILL PUBLISHING HOUSE
B-9, Rattan Jyoti, 18 Rajendra Place,
New Delhi - 110 008 (INDIA)
Tel. : 5750801, 5755519
Fax : 5763428

Ist Published 1998
Reprint 1998

© Publishers

Printed at Kumar Offset Printers, Delhi - 110 031

T. Kusalakumar
BEng (Hons) MBA MAPM MCIM
Project Manager

PREFACE

The concept of education has changed and so the conception of errors in writing and speaking English. Correct English is no longer as important as good English but good English is not always correct English! Many errors are permissible if these do not hinder the cultivation of soul, correct thinking, and exchange ideas.

An understanding of common errors in English is important to the extent these help us to think and to express our ideas concisely and precisely.

This is a book on common, current and popular errors in the writing and speaking of English. It does not concern itself with uncommon and extraordinary mistakes which are above the comprehension of an average student and beyond the common man's horizon of understanding.

Many grammatical errors, which were regarded as mistakes in the past, are no longer looked upon as such. Many deviations of grammar are now tolerated which were frowned upon even as much as a quarter of a century before. Such mistakes do not form the scope of this book.

Half the mistakes that the modern users of English commit, are merely mistakes of spelling. So special attention has been paid to mistakes in spelling and special practice exercises have been included for that purpose.

This common book deals with most of the common mistakes the common men commit in their common use of English in their common life.

—MICHAEL BRAGANZA

CONTENTS

1

INTRODUCTION

Common Errors in English are very common indeed. Even the top writers are likely to make the errors of omission and commission in the off-guarded moment. In order to write good and perfect English one has to be careful all the time. Any slip of pen or tongue can damage the reputation of a man—or raise a laughter!

Hearty and Heart-felt

Once I committed a serious mistake at Simla. I had gone to the house of my friend Mr. Ram Paul, I.A.S. to pay my condolences to him on the death of his mother. He not being at home, I left a note paying my "heartiest sympathies" to him in his great bereavement. I wrote the note in haste and did not care to revise the words that I used.

When he met me a couple of months later in Delhi, he was terribly angry. He said the word should have been "heart-felt" instead of "heartiest".

Personally, I do not see much difference between "heartiest" and "heart-felt" because both mean coming from the heart. And "heartiest" perhaps means deeper than mere "heart-felt". But most of the people prefer the latter: and we have to respect the susceptibilities of the common usage.

The true value of a word does not depend on what the people think it means. So, we should go by the common usage.

Changing use of words

The use and sense of many words change not only in the course of a generation but even in a few years and sometimes even in a few months.

Many words which meant something very good at one time do not mean the same thing now. Take, for example, the word "Capitalist". It was not a bad word before Karl Marx ran it down to the ground and made it a term of abuse. Now to call somebody a "capitalist" is to call him names, but in actual use of the sense the word is not bad at all.

Similarly at one time "Scribbler" was a decent word for a writer. But now to call a writer as "Scribbler" is to abuse him.

Therefore, the right principle in correct English is "Watch your words". You have to be conscious and careful about the kind of words you are using and about the kind of people you are using them for.

Correct Spellings

The correct spelling of the words that you use in your writing are most important. A wrong word can destroy in the dust the impression of an otherwise excellent piece of writing.

Disaster overtakes your literary piece when the wrong spelling of one word leads to the making of an entirely new word.

For example:

Piece for peace

Effect for affect

Pray for prey

Look at the ludicrous effect if you say, "My friend was *preying* in the temple". That can be damaging to his reputation. Some people might think he was robbing the gods or hunting for girls!

You must make a habit of examining the correct spelling of every word you employ; and, if you are not sure of its spelling, you should look it up in the dictionary. Only a regular habit of reference forth and back will make you perfect in the art of correct English.

Aglore and Galore

Sometimes one can commit a mistake unconsciously for months and years without being aware of it, because other people may not be aware of the mistake too, and so it may continue and sometimes even give rise to an entirely new word. Most of Shakespearean word were born that way. He used many words not being fully aware of their spellings, sense and significance. In the course of time these words have become new additions to the English dictionary.

I have also been using the word "Aglore" quite often in my writings for the press and the word passed without anybody pointing out to me that the spelling of the word was wrong. This is due to the fact that the word is not in common use and few people bother to look up the meaning of the words they use or read in the journal and newspaper.

One day I was pleasantly shocked when Mr. Cecil, the good old artist of the Indian Observer, pointed out to me that there was no such word as "Aglore" in the dictionary; and that the word should be "galore". It means "in abundance". He was right!

Correct writing is such a delicate thing that unless we are careful of the time about all the words that we are using, we are likely to commit ludicrous and sometimes serious mistakes.

Dictionary Habit

You must keep a dictionary always handy and make dictionary-using a lifelong habit. Any doubt about meaning or spelling of words should be immediately checked up.

Even the greatest writers constantly consult the dictionary to protect themselves against possible mistakes. Nobody can be a perfect writer or even a good correct writer without backing or banking on the storehouse of knowledge that is treasured in the dictionary. It embodies the wisdom of the sages and the ages from all times and climes.

By constant use you will soon realize that the use of a dictionary is easy and pleasant. It adds to your word-power and correct usage. By looking for old words, you also come across new words and thus you go on adding to your storehouse of knowledge.

It is a good habit to look into the dictionary casually when you are not looking for any particular word. By that method you can improve your English by constantly adding new words and shades of meanings depicted in them.

Use of Grammar

Grammar is now occupying less and less important a position in the thinking of the modern writers and nobody bothers about grammatical rules so long as you can convey your meaning correctly and forcefully, but you are supposed to have elementary knowledge of grammatical rules so as not to confuse your thinking and your writing.

There are complicated rules of grammar which can be ignored and glossed over; but there are some primary and fundamental rules which have to be carefully looked after. For example, if you mix up "is" with "was" and "will", you confuse the tenses and thereby fail to convey your idea to the readers and the listeners.

By breaking the fundamental rules of grammar, our ideas become wrong, the sentences become erroneous and we stand self-condemned.

Grammar is not merely the science of correct writing but it is also the essence of right thinking. Grammar is the logic of language as logic is the grammar of thinking.

Journalese

New kinds of words and sentences are now being used in journals and newspapers. These words and sentences are not always grammatically correct, but these are now becoming popular because of the effect created on the minds of the readers.

These innovations cannot be called breaches of the grammatical rules or other laws of correct writing and should not be mistaken for wrong English. These are now permissible in all countries of the world and should be understood and tolerated.

These make the language lively. New forms and words are being created to add new dimensions to the language. For example, "Nope" is now used as a single word for "No hope". Similarly, "from can-see to can't see" has been used to mean "from morning to evening" by Negro writers. There is also a new word "stick-activeness", which means determination and resolution to see a thing through to its success.

Indianisms

Many Indianisms are coming into use. These are idioms and phrases peculiar to the users of English in India. Although these are technically and grammatically wrong, these should not be taken for mistakes. It is best to tolerate them unless they are so flagrant that they make a nonsense of the English language.

English

English is now almost an Indian English, this impact of Indian mind and character on the use of English is a natural development and should be welcomed.

For example: The right idiom is:

"Not to speak of one rupee, I do not have even a paisa in my pocket".

But most of the common users of English in India will say:

"What to speak of a rupee, I do not have even a paisa in my pocket".

This form is now being so widely used in India even by school-masters and office superintendents that it will be grammatical rule on the Indian soil.

Illegibility

It must be remembered that illegible writing is the cause of many mistakes that occur in the language. Some top scholars like Robert Browning wrote so illegibly that they themselves could not understand what they had written. Robert Browning's fault, of course, was not so much illegibility as vagueness and confusion. When friends asked him the meaning of certain lines, he is known to have said, "God and I knew when the poem was written what it meant. But now only God knows what it means"!

Some scholars and students who are not sure of their spellings and words deliberately write illegibly so that no one may know whether they are writing correctly or wrongly. But it is a great error of thinking, except in the case of doctors who are proverbially illegible. One can find out whether the man is trying to cheat the reader by trying to be illegible or not. The students who practise this kind of cheating in the examinations seldom get good marks.

But doctors are the most notorious in this kind of illegible writing. Giving a formula of success to a doctor who was not of this ilk, his wife told him why he was starving. She said to him for making money in his practice:

"You should write your bills legibly but your prescriptions illegibly".

There is another joke about a man who received a letter from a doctor friend and found it so illegible that he had to seek the help of a druggist. But the latter, instead of reading out the personal letter to him, handed over a medicine to him:

"That will cost you £ 10".

The man laughed and went home!

2

WORDS LIKELY TO
BE MISSPELT

There are lots of words which are likely to be misspelt and you should pay special care in spelling them out.

Here is a short list that will prove handy to you.

Arrive, arrival

Arrange, arrangement

Judge, judgement

Fit, fitting

Write, writing, written

Receive, device, achieve

Edit, editor

Advice, adviser

Junior, senior, inferior, superior, ulterior

Prefer, preferred

Concur, concurred

Hear, heard

Come, coming

Light, lighting, lightning

Red, read

Lead, led

Forget, forgettable

Comfort, comfortable

Delightful, delightfully

Beauty, beautifully

Command, commend
Precis, precise
Stationery, stationary
Prophesy, prophecy
Practise, practice
Fell, felled
Lay, laid, lain
Boast, boost
Kite, tight
Prey, pray
Rot, thought, taut, taught
Reason, season
Time, rhyme
Work, jerk, lurk
Conductor, curator, prosecutor
Sovereignty
Christianity
Christen, Christian
Ant, aunt
Counsel, council
Restaurant
Library
Doctor
Electricity

Machine, mechanic, mechanical
Engine, engineer
Revolution, evolution
Evaporate
Exercise, exorcise
Intrinsic, extrinsic
Interior, exterior
Expedite
Existence
Extravagance
Expedient
Favour, favourite, favourable, favouritism
Feasible, possible, practicable
Passable, possible, impossible
Feature, picture
Photo, photograph, photography, photographer
Facility, felicity
Feminine, masculine
Fence, fencing, fencible
Fetch
Often
Usually

Feast, festive, festival

Five, fifth, fifteen, fifty

Nine, ninth, nineteen, ninety

Finger, figure

Fill, full, fulfil, fulfilled

Find, fined

Affect, effect

Finance, financier, financial

Gait, gate

Cease, seize

Analyse, analysis

Synthesis, synthesize

Why

Ocean, motion

Dictate, dictator, dictation

Stenography, typewriting

Office, routine

Sympathy, sympathetic

Herd, heard, hard

Ignorance

Conscious, conscience

Jury, jurisdiction

Jest, just

Kangaroo

Boomerang

Occasion

Accommodation

Obvious

Accident

Incident

Occupy, occupation

Penalty, penalise

Casualty, casualness

Casual, causal

Receive, reception

Reciprocal

Recite, recital

Retaliate

Rite, write, right

Raise, raze

See, sea

Seen, scene

So, sow

3

THE RIGHT USE
OF WORDS

It is important to understand the right meaning and the right use of words to eliminate common errors from your writing. Some of the serious errors creep in because we lack proper meaning of the word which we use in our daily correspondence.

In order to write good and correct English, it is important to learn good words and understand their meaning.

Is it possible to hold one arm akimbo? Whenever that word is used in novels, the character is always said to have his arms akimbo.

The "word" means to have a hand on the hip with the elbow turned outward, so why does it always have to be used in the plural?

That question and those delicious words were scribbled more than a year ago on a yellow piece of paper pinned to a cork board. The idea was to make a list of great words, ones that were either so precise in meaning that they could never be misused or so mouthfilling that it was a joy to utter them.

One of the most precise words in the language never gets the use it deserves. "Defenestrate" means to throw someone or something out of a window. It was an old Bohemian custom to throw nasty people out of the window. When a group of Protestant Bohemians so rid themselves of two of their Emperor's envoys, that event–called the Defenestration of Prague—started the Thirty Years' War. It was, in its time, as world shaking an event as the bombing of Pearl Harbour. Yet the word has almost disappeared from the language. Who has ever read an account of local residents defenestrating the garbage?

You'd think that all of those busily defenestrating citizens would have brought the word back into use "Berm," for example, was rescued from the scarp heap by the needs of a modern sport. Originally it meant either the path along the top of a dike or any narrow shelf passage or ledge. Now it's a popular word among motorcycle racers.

When racing bikes go around a corner on a dirty track, they throw dirt to the outer edge of the turn. This "berm" then becomes the fastest way through the turn. And the racers talk of riding the berm.

It's not the meaning of the word that makes it attractive; it's the funny sound. Imagine someone saying: "hey, Charlie, that's a fine berm out there" or "I was going great until I got bumped on the berm".

Computer experts use a marvellously appropriate word to describe a fault in a system. They call it a "glitch". This may not be a precise description of the problem, but it has the advantage of sounding bad. And when something as complicated as a computer goes wrong, the word to describe the happening should have a certain pungency. "Glitch" has an enormously satisfying nastiness.

"Wan" is a word that gets written often but you seldom hear anyone trying to pronounce it. It means sick or feeble, and it's hard to say the word in any way that doesn't sound just like that.

"Onomatopoeia" is a great word in itself. It sounds like the opening rhythms of a spirited Croatian folk dance, and it's diverting to say just for the sound of it. But it also describes a class of words that may be the most fun for all. These are words, such as 'buzz' and 'hiss' that imitate the sounds of the things they describe. How about "susurrous" to describe the whispering of the wind in the trees? Or "tintinnabulation" an old word given broad currency by Edgar Allen Poe when he used it to describe the sound of bells?

Those are high-class examples of onomatopoeia. A couple of the best ones still haven't made it beyond the dictionaries of slang "Barf", as a description of the end result of the process of reverse peristalsis has a certain crude power. But perhaps the best description of that process was written by the man who had just completed an airline trip through rough air. He said he spent the flight shouting "O'rouke" into an airsick bag.

The act of being gullible does not have a distinctive sound. But if it did, the sound would clearly fall on the ear as "gullible". The sound of the word is perfectly matched to the foolishness it defines.

A colleague of mine sometimes uses the truly elegant word "gravamen". It refers to the significant portion of a grievance or complaint. It's the kind of word that comes clothed in black judicial robes and moves into a sentence to the grand march from "Aida". It's a word that could transform a hangnail from a complaint into a cause.

"Ampersand" has to be included on any list of great words as an example of much ado about nothing. The ampersand is nothing more than the symbol '&' which means nothing more than "and".

Why should such a simple concept be expressed with such a pretentious word? It sounds like something that would be inclined to crawl under a rock to mate with a gerrymander, which incidentally is another fine word that meets a real need. Without it, trying to describe politics would be a great deal more difficult if not impossible.

Among the terms used in the punctuation of the language, the comma is the most aptly named. It would, for example, seem appropriate to name a microscopic creature that had a shape of that punctuation make a "comma".

The hyphen and the dash, unfortunately, somehow got mixed. A hyphen sounds fat like a dash; and a dash sounds thin, like a hyphen.

Depending on the context the mark "colon" can also be used to describe a dismal portion of the anatomy. And speaking of the colon, why is it given full credit for the paternity of the semicolon? That little creature could just as easily be called a semi-comma.

4

WATCH YOUR WORDS

It is bad if the spelling of a word you use is bad. It is worse if the word with the wrong spelling makes a new word with ludicrous effect. It is worst possible if using a word with a wrong spelling you run into business losses.

The classical example of the worst mistake due to wrong spelling occurred some years back in a circular issued by an American insurance company. The Managing Director did not find it profitable to invite a certain type of insurance and dictated a note to the possible clients. He dictated : "Any further policies will not be effected".

The Lady Secretary, not more intelligent than the boss, typed the note as "Any further policies will not be affected".

The boss signed the letter without caring to note whether the word typed was "effected" or "affected". The company suffered a loss of $ 100,000 before the mistake was spotted. And it was Managing Director who was dismissed, not the Secretary.

It was his duty to read the letter very carefully and correct it before putting his signature on it.

1. The minister said that the church widows were a disgrace to the parish and it was time somebody washed them. ☒

   —*Examiner, San Francisco*

   Say "windows" not "widows". ☑

2. A 36 year old New York school teacher became the bride of a 77 year old New York minister and the father of nine children. —*Star, Kansas City, U.S.A.* ☒

   Say "bride", not "pride". ☑

3. Rushing to her room, Lousie dressed in paste and joined him in his car. Neither of them spoke. —*News, Arizona, Texas* ☒

   Say "haste", not "paste". ☑

4. Mr. and Mrs. Frank Dipierro, of Miles Avenue, are receiving congratulations on the birth of a daughter. Both mother and baby are doing well under the car of Dr. Robert Sievers. ☒

   Say "care", not "car". ☑

5. She used an ordinary rod, and light tickle. ☒

   —*News, Freeport, U.S.A.*

Say "tackle", not "tickle". ☑

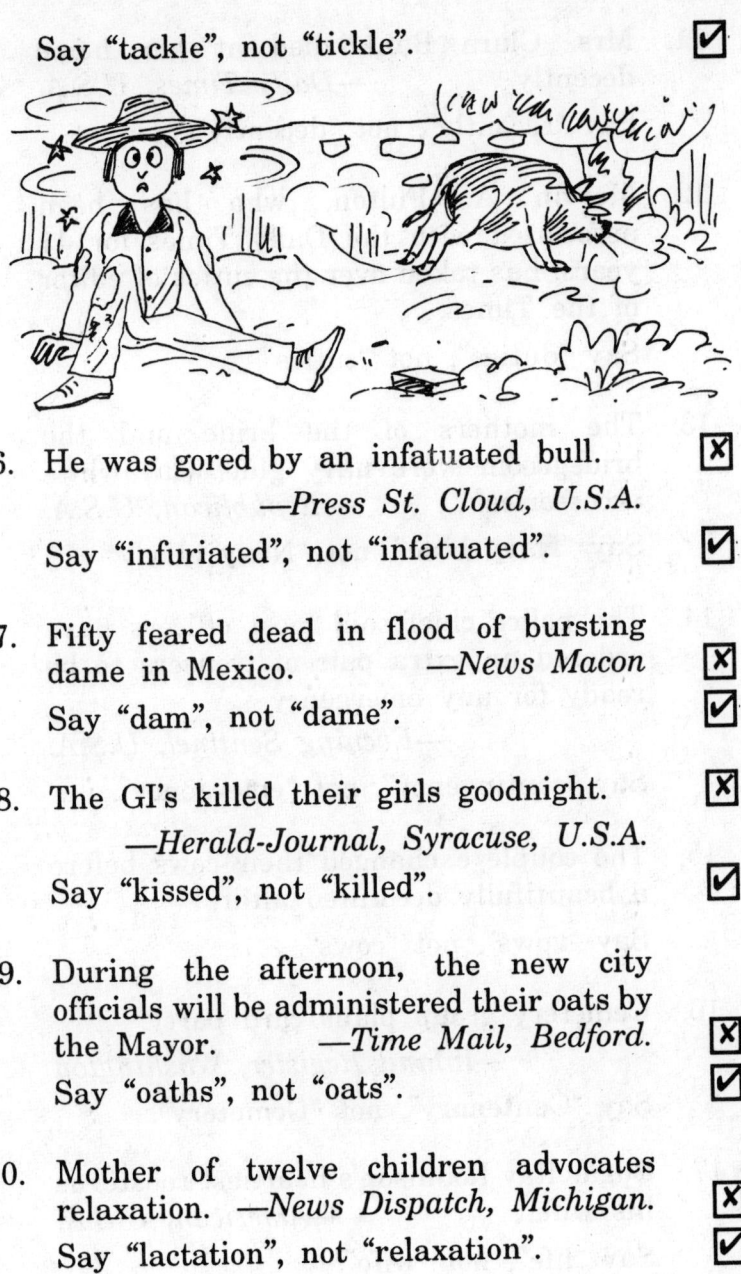

6. He was gored by an infatuated bull. ☒
   —*Press St. Cloud, U.S.A.*
   Say "infuriated", not "infatuated". ☑

7. Fifty feared dead in flood of bursting
   dame in Mexico.   —*News Macon* ☒
   Say "dam", not "dame". ☑

8. The GI's killed their girls goodnight. ☒
   —*Herald-Journal, Syracuse, U.S.A.*
   Say "kissed", not "killed". ☑

9. During the afternoon, the new city
   officials will be administered their oats by
   the Mayor.   —*Time Mail, Bedford.* ☒
   Say "oaths", not "oats". ☑

10. Mother of twelve children advocates
    relaxation. —*News Dispatch, Michigan.* ☒
    Say "lactation", not "relaxation". ☑

11. Mrs. Clara Bank died at her home decently.   —*Daily Times, U.S.A.* ☒ ☑

Say "recently", not "decently".

12. Mervin A. Fulton, who has been associated with the Daily Times for 41 years, has taken over the cuties of editor of the Times. ☒ ☑

Say "duties", not "cuties".

13. The mothers of the bride and the bridegroom wore navy glue with white accessories.   —*Republican, U.S.A.* ☒ ☑

Say "Navy blue", not "Navy glue".

14. The police chief said most officers have ordered an extra pair of trousers to be ready for any emergency. ☒

        —*Evening Sentinel, U.S.A.*

Say "contingency", not "emergency". ☑

15. The couple exchanged their cows before a beautifully decorated altar. ☒ ☑

Say "vows", not "cows".

16. Cemetery group plans card party. ☒

        —*Inland Register, Washington*

Say "Centenary", not "Cemetery". ☑

17. Sugar Ray Robinson's heartiest rooster is his wife.   —*American, U.S.A.* ☒

Say "life", not "wife". ☑

18. Woman complained to OPS after the Cleveland Trust Co. raised its assessment on bed checks from 50 cents to a dollar. ☒

—*Beacon Journal, Ohio.*

Say "bad cheques", not "bed checks". ☑

19. The buried man emerged from his trap near the seaport of Gadynia recently with a kneelength beard and hair hanging down to his angles. ☒

—*New Telegraph, U.S.A.*

Say "ankles", not "angles". ☑

5

EVERYDAY ERRORS

There are errors which most of us commit because we often become puzzled and cannot make up our mind as to which is the correct word, meaning or spelling. For example, often we cannot decide between 'Receive' and 'Recieve' as the right word. Such difficulties should be immediately referred to the dictionary to clear the dust from the mirrors of our minds.

Announcement

Correct the following announcement:

Awl tenagers (those abowe ten yeers old and belou tweenty years old) in V-Bloke rajouri garden, new delhi 127 or rekwested to right out the fallowing informashun abouvt themselves, and deeliver to the undersined far a very impartont meating:

1. Fool Name.
2. Number off the house.

3. Berth daet (or approximete aje if berth daet naught avleabel).

4. Profestion (if a stodent, stait the sckool or colej and thee closs).

5. Intreerist, ambishion otr aspperation in life.

This informotion, writen on paper, shuld be suplied too the undersined immediately or withen three das at the lattest.

Corrected version

All teenagers (those above ten years old and below twenty years old) in V-Block (both the wings) of Rajouri Garden, New Delhi-27, are requested to write out the following information about themselves, and deliver to the undersigned for a very important meeting:

1. Full name

2. Number of the House

3. Birth date (or approximate age if birth date is not available)

4. Profession (if a student, state the school or college and the class)

5. Interest, ambition or aspiration in life.

This information, written on paper, should be supplied to the undersigned IMMEDIATELY or WITHIN THREE DAYS at the latest.

Deliberations:

CAPITOL PUNISHMENT

Living in the capitol of India today is a capitole punishment.

Eeerly at daun, beefore daybrake, you can hung riund a melk-buth, and as well hujd a giyt a botle of melk.

Lait at dosk, after nite fal—and that is a day-lung storey,—you can hong on a Delhi Transport Corporation bus, and it is easier to hang yoorself or geet under its wheils than get unto a buss!

Dooring the day, your mathers, wives and dauters may heng round a rashun shap til sunset, because shatters wil neaver go up beefore these come doown upon them.

Soogar is bitter; and poisoneous adalterated floor grantees a long lengering deeth Qoite paneful ekspenshive affalre Henging bye the fun assoores a kwick comfartable despozal.

In any cause, your seiling fun is good only far hunging, because of electric brakedowns and shortages, you can expect a greem hangman's somer.

Go to any government office to execute any business whatsoever, and you find it is full of executioners.

At the booking windows of Indian Railways and Air India, they now ishu tikets only for the ether warld.

Corrected Version:

CAPITAL PUNISHMENT

Living in the capital of India today is a capital punishment.

Early at dawn, before daybreak, you can hang round a milk-booth, and as well get hanged to get a bottle of milk.

Late at dusk, after nightfall—and that is a day-long story—you can hang on a Delhi Transport Corporation bus, and it is easier to hang yourself or get under its wheels than get into a bus!

During the day, your mothers, wives and daughters may hang round a ration shop till sunset, because shutters will never go up before these come down upon them.

Sugar is bitter; and poisonous adulterated flour guarantees a long lingering death. Quite painful expensive affair. Hanging by the fan assures a quick comfortable disposal.

In any case, your ceiling fan is good only for hanging, because of electric breakdowns and shortages, you can expect a grim hangman's summer.

Go to any government office to execute any business whatsoever, and you find it is full of executioners.

At the booking windows of Indian Railways and Air India, they now issue tickets only for the other world.

Deliberation:

NIVER LOCK BECK AT BOOTY

Niver lock beck to reasses and redmire bewty,
Far bewty is niver the some as the second lock
What you fend that the first lock
Niver the same at the third lock.
War it is at the second lock
Bewty changes in the twenkling of an eye
The bewtifool buoy flys,
The goolden ger, I takes vinggs.
We change perpetwally,
And perpetwally become different men.
We or never the same even a secand after.
We or all ways becoming diferent
Frame what wee wear a while ago,
Their is naught won whole man
Their are millions of men
Inside a single man,
We air all ways diffarent and yet the same
We are all ways the same and yet differeant
Or their mirors in space
Depicting Won Bewty—
Only Won Beeing, —
Mirrors with multipupose seeing?

Corrected Version:

NEVER LOOK BACK AT BEAUTY

Never look back to reassess and readmire beauty,
For beauty will be flown,
Beauty is never the same at the second look
What you find it at the first look,
Never the same at the third look
What it is at the second look,
Beauty changes in the twinkling of an eye
The beautiful boy flies,
The golden girl takes wings.
We change perpetually,
And perpetually become different men,
We are never the same even a second after.
We are always becoming different
From what we were a while ago!
There is not one whole man
There are millions of men
Inside a single man,
As outside a single man!
We are always different and yet the same,
We are always the same and yet different.
Are there mirrors in space
Depicting One Beauty—
Only one Being,—
Mirrors with multipurpose seeing?

Sonnet

I GAMBOL WITH THE STARS

I gambol weth thee stars which are may dice,
And Son Hemsilg is my brtitest thrower:
I gambol weth the unevirse, my douer
My life's a golden gambol wisch is so nice
My highesr staiks are virchu and vice,
A kosmick spurt in witch noting's lower
Or higher then the petles of a floweur.
While jiewels and diemands a or butt trice.
My Friend! pley, pley up, pley up the game :
Concentrate awl and ever thing you staik;
When without honour and loose withot shame;
Your vicktory is naught far your own sake:
Farget yourself too remeber brathers;
Yor pley far the enjayment of others,

Corrected Version:
Sonnet

I GAMBLE WITH THE STARS

I gamble with the stars which are my dice,
And Sun Himself is my brightest thrower,
I gamble with the universe, my dower,
My life's a golden gamble which is so nice,
My highest stakes are virtue and the vice,

A cosmic sport in which nothing's lower,
Or higher than the petals of a flower,
While jewels and diamonds are but trice
My Friend! play up, play up, play up the game;
Concentrate all and everything you stake;
Win without honour and lose without shame;
Your Victory is not for your own sake;
Forget yourself to remember brothers;
You play for the enjoyment of others.

—*Jagat S. Bright*

Correct the following:

DADA T.L. VASWANI

For over half sentury Dadji T.L. Vaswami hes bye present and praktise champiened the cause of the dumb, defesels creachers. To him thiese VOISELES WONES or members of the WON GRATE FEMELY OFF GODD. He uffecskunataitely kall them Over Yonger Brathers and Sesters.

Is awl life is Sacred have been brot together sum of the uterences and rightings of this grait mistic hamintarian. These thoyts have sprang frame thee hart of a hooly man of God a hart with is toched witch sarrow at the crewlties man has inflicted on domn defenceless creachers, Every ward is a penetrating and peerces the hart and well. We trost, awakan the reeder too his dooties and reponseebeelities toowiords the "speachless world".

"We breethe out an aspeeration that yhe bouk may bee so blesed as too kindel inn sum harts littel kandels of *compation and draw many to the grate trooth that awl life is sacred*".

—*Gangaram Sajandas*

GOD'S MIMAAJ

I heave scene Gods imaaj in berds and beesys, I heave learnt off them lessens witch heave drawn my hart neerer to trooth and luve. And one of the greatest aspirations of my lief is too be spint mour and mour in the sirvece of these younger brathers and sesters in thee won Grait Feemily of Hem whu liuves awl lief.

THE WORLD'S NEED

Anue awkning is thee warld's pitieous nead twoday. O'for suns and dauters of Krishna and Krist, of Budda and Mahavira, of Nanak and Frances, to revel a nue beiwty of reverance far lief—suns and dauters who wuld renoncing gread and grateness, bee among the sirvents of anemles nd homanetly.

NEW PATRIOTS

I heve tryed, inn a humbel way, to stody the strugle off centories far homan rites, for hamun lebirasion. And eye heve boed two the patriats and marters of hamunity.

"Ween well the dey come when the grate ones of humanity may bee banded together for the seervice of the aneemle world.

Corrected Versions:

DADA T.L. VASWANI

For over half a century, Dadaji Shri T.L. Vaswani has by precept and practice championed the cause of dumb, defenceless creatures. To him these 'VOICELESS ONES', are 'members of the ONE GREAT FAMILY OF GOD'. He affectionately calls them our younger brothers and sisters.

In all Life is Sacred have been brought together some of the utterances and writings of this great mystic humanitarian. These thoughts have sprung from the heart of a holy man of God,—a heart which is touched with sorrow at the cruelties, man has inflicted on dumb defenceless creatures. Every word is penetrating and pierces the heart and will. We trust, it will awaken the reader to his duties and responsibilities towards the 'speechless world'.

We breathe out an aspiration that the book may be so blessed as to kindle in some hearts little candles of compassion and draw many to the great truth that all life is sacred.

—*Gangaram Sajandas*

GOD'S IMAGE

I have seen God's image shining in birds and beasts. I have learnt of them lessons which have drawn my heart nearer to truth and love. And one of the greatest aspirations of my life is to be spent more and more in the service of these younger brothers and sisters in the one Great Family of Him who loves all life.

THE WORLD'S NEED

A new awakening is the world's piteous need today. O! for sons and daughters of KRISHNA and CHRIST, of BUDDHA and MAHAVIRA, of NANAK and FRANCIS to reveal a new beauty of reverence for life,—sons and daughters who would, renouncing greed and greatness, be among the servants of animals and humanity.

NEW PATRIOTS

I have tried, in a humble way, to study the struggle of centuries for human rights, for human liberation. And I have bowed to the patriots and martyrs of humanity.

"When will the day come—the day when the great ones of humanity may be bound together for the service of the animal world"?

Correct the following:

A FEEST FAR THEE BERDS

Eye heave again and again thot off Godd as thee vgrait Brather and Barden-beerer and Beest.

Thees humbrl creachers tahil far us and wee dair there rites deny.

St. Francis odf Assisi—Apostle of compation and luve—expressed a thot on which eye heave luved to mediate again and again.

"If eye can speak to the Emperar, eye well beeg heim too maik a universal edikt, oblijing awl thees who heave the meens too spreed rice and grane a long the raods, that thee beerds espeshally our sesters, the larks, shoold heave a feest".

LVE AND LIT LEVE's a sublimbly solman mesage was given to us by the Lord Mahavira about 2,500 yeers aggo. It has been highly approved bye awl the religions dignatories sinse than. The Gospal of Mercy and Charety of Lard Jesus Krist is butt anather vershion of the shame imartle law. Gautam Buddha and profit Mohammed Sahib produced the shame luvin kindness and benignity. Lord Krishna in the Gita preeched the shame generusity and kindly fealing towards awl. Who has naught hart of Guru Nank Sahib's kindliness eaven to berds and animals?

A poet like Shakespeare putt the shame theim in his peotikal fansy:

The quality of mercy is naught
It dropeth as the gentel haven,
It blesseth heim that geeves and heem that taeekas.

To donate to

CHAREETY BIRDS HASPEETLE AND SELINT HALPERS BRATHERHUD

is a rite step on the puth of mangnonimos merxy.

"How happy wooled eye feel if awl the mares of the seeties and all the lards of the cashless and toons woold solemanly promise every year on the day, sacred as the berth day of our lard, to induse there man to do one thing—to throw their wheat and their grain a long the roods beyond the ceeties and walved toons so that our sisters, the larks and ether berds have planty to eat."

Correct Version:

A FEAST FOR THE BIRDS

I have again and again thought of God as the great Brother and Burden-bearer of bird and beast.

These humble creatures toil for us and we dare deny their rights!

St. Francis of Assisi—Apostle of compassion and love— expressed a thought on which I have loved to meditate again and again:

"If I can speak to the Emperor, I will beg him to make a Universal edict, obliging all those who have the means to spread rice and grain along the roads, that the birds, especially our sisters, the larks should have a feast".

'LIVE AND LET LIVE' a sublimely solemn message was given to us by Lord Mahavira about 2,500 years ago. It has been highly approved by all the religious dignitaries since then. The Gospel of Mercy and Charity of Lord Jesus Christ is but another version of the same immortal Law. Gautam Buddha and Prophet Mohammad Sahib produced the same loving kindness and benignity. Lord Krishna in the Gita preached the same generosity and kind feelings

42

towards all. Who has not heard of Guru Nanak Sahib's kindliness even to birds and animals?

A poet like Shakespeare put the same theme in his poetical fancy:

The quality of Mercy is not strained.

It droppeth as the gentle rain from heaven

It blesseth him that gives and him that takes

To donate to—

CHARITY BIRDS HOSPITAL AND SILENT HELPERS BROTHERHOOD

is a right step on the path of magnanimous mercy.

"How happy would I feel if all the mayors of the cities and all the lords of the castles and towns would solemnly promise every year on the day, sacred as the birthday of our Lord, to induce their men to do one thing—to throw their wheat and their grain along the roads beyond the cities and walled towns, so that our sisters, the larks, and other birds may have plenty to eat".

6

WRONG USE OF RIGHT WORDS

It often happens that you know the right use of a word, but your sentence is so hastily drafted without attention to punctuations and right place of words that the effect is ludicrous if it is not tragic, causing you losses and conveying quite the reverse of the sense and shade you have in the mind.

examples:

1. The Nebraska Legislature was asked to enact a law providing annulment of marriages of all couples who do not within three years after the wedding day have one or more children by Representative Hines, Democrat of Omaha, who is bachelor and next to the youngest member of the Assembly. ☒

   The Nebraska Legislature was asked by Representative Hines, Democrat of

Omaha, who is a bachelor and next to the youngest member of the Assembly, to enact a law providing annulment of marriages of all couples who do not have one or more children within three years after the wedding day. ☑

2. Mrs. Grace Wright is being wired for electricity which will be a great improvement and add considerably to her value in the community. ☒

—*Sentinel, Ohio*

A wire is being sent to Mrs. Grace Wright for electricity which will be a great improvement and add considerably to her value in the community. ☑

3. New Sultan of Morocco, entitled to four wives, prefer monogamy. ☒

—*Bee, News, U.S.A.*

New Sultan of Morocco, entitled to four wives, prefers monogamy. ☑

4. A bathroom shower was given the bride ☒

—*News, New York*

The bride was given a bathroom shower. ☑

5. Boy hit by tractor, plow is hospitalised ☒

—*News Sun, Ohio*

The boy, hit by tractor plow, is hospitalized. ☑

6. Story quoting the director of the Miss Canada Pageant, stating that girls will be judged in evening dresses rather than bathing suits: "I have fought for five years to get bathing suits of the girls". ☒

   —*Kitchener, Waterloo*

   He should have said, "I have fought for five years to have the girls judged in evening dresses and not bathing suits". ☑

7. With or without a bathing suit Barbara Blank is a mighty pretty girl. ☒

   —*Evening Monitor, Texas.*

   In a bathing suit or otherwise, Barbara Blank is a mighty pretty girl. ☑

8. When she washes dishes, he should wash dishes with her and when she mops up the floor, he should mop up the floor with her. —*Western Family Magazine* ☒

   When she washes dishes, he should wash dishes along with her; and when she mops up the floor, he should mop up the floor along with her. ☑

9. John Blank passed away last week. Our best wishes to him for a speedy recovery. ☒

   —*Times, Texas*

   John Blank passed this way last week. Our best wishes to him for a speedy recovery. ☑

10. Man found shot to death by car. ☒

Man by the car found shot to death. ☑

11. Joan Crawford plans to become woman producer. ☒

Joan Crawford plans to become a producer woman. ☑

12. Mingling of sexes in college favoured, 18 to 7, by girls at Boston Lying-in Hospital. ☒
—*Traveller, Boston*

Mingling of sexes in college favoured by girls at Boston Lying-in Hospital by 18 to 7. ☑

13. Woman, 30, dies; may live here. ☒
—*Journal Albuquerque*

Woman, 30, may live here or die. ☑

7

ADVERTISEMENT ATROCITIES

Advertisements are often full of great errors of omission or commission, often causing a ludicrous situation and sometimes resulting in losses and misunderstandings by the clients and would-be customers. Here are a few examples.

For sale

A bull-blooded cow giving milk; three tons of hay, lot of chickens; several stoves. ☒

A full-blooded cow, giving milk, three tons of hay, lots of chickens, and several stoves. ☑

To Let

2 lovely room, suitable 2 women, delightful advance. ☒

Two lovely rooms with delightful approaches suitable for two women to let. ☑

Wanted

Have an immediate opening for a first class stenographer, preferable one with little business experience. ☒

Have an immediate opening for a first class stenographer, preferably one with a little business experience. ☑

Worker having less Children

Wanted—Reliable orchard man for steady job. Don't have more than two children if you can help it. ☒

Wanted—Reliable orchard man for a steady job, having preferably not more than two children. ☑

Stale Eggs

We have the same eggs for sale that we have last summer. Come and see us. ☒

We have the eggs of the same quality for sale that we had last year. Come and see us. ☑

Auctioneer

Auctioneering is my special line of business. Prices are very reasonable. If I am out of town, make dates with my wife. ☒

If I am out of town, my wife will give you an appointment with me. ☑

House to Rent

House to rent by a widow newly painted and renovated with every modern improvement. ☒

A widow renting out a house newly painted and renovated with every modern improvement. ☑

Experience

Wanted Grocery clerk, experience unnecessary but essential. ☒

Wanted—Grocery clerk, experience not necessary but desirable. ☑

8

KNAVES OF
THE NOTICE BOARD

Often English given on the notice board is wrong. Sometimes it has quite a wrong meaning due to wrong arrangement of words. Here and there they are ludicrous. Now and then these are disastrous. This is not only true in India but even of notice boards put up in England and U.S.A. Here are some examples of silly notice boards in America.

1. Eat Here and Get Gas

Literally it means take your food and die. To "give gas" means to give poisonous gas which the Nazis used to give to their enemies.

The right wording should be: "Eat Here And Get Gas for Your Car".

2. Hangover Breakfast

In Nashville, the Hide-Away Restaurant there has the notice-board: "Hangover Breakfast—Tomato-juice,

Raw Eggs, Aspirin, Black Coffee, Our Deepest Sympathy".

This is quite wrong. "Hangover Breakfast" would mean a breakfast that will hang you. It should rather be called "Standing Breakfast" or "Buffet Breakfast". Again to mix up "Aspirin" with other items is quite wrong. To use "Our deepest sympathy" would mean as if it is a condolence service after death due to the killing breakfast. It should be "Our best service".

3. Thank You—Come Again Next Year!

In a Maternity Hospital in Vermont, U.S.A. there is a notice: "Thank you—Come Again Next Year". This refers to the fact of nature that a child is born once a year. But the idea is just silly. It should simply be: "Thank you. Come again when you need our service".

4. Do Not Drive In When the Doors Are Shut

This is a notice on a garage in Seattle, Washington. The idea is just silly. How can you drive in when the doors are shut? It should rather be "Do Not Drive In When We Have Closed".

5. Laundry Laughter

In a laundry shop in U.S.A., there is a sign:

"We Do Not Tear Your Cloth With Machinery. We Do It Carefully By Hand".

It means that the laundry shop does not tear your clothes by machinery but tears them carefully with the hand. The sign should be:

"We Do Not Tear Your Cloth By Machinery. We Wash Them Carefully By Hand".

6. Fresh Fish Walk In

This sign along an Ohio road is just silly. It means as if fishes are walking inside the hotel. There should be a fullstop between the two ideas. Thus:

"Fresh Fish. Walk In".

7. Aroma One Half Mile

This is Indiana road sign in U.S.A. There should be dash after Aroma. Thus "Aroma—One and a Half Mile".

8. No Bicycle Riding Dogs

There is a sign in Ashbury Park in U.S.A. — "No Bicycle Riding Dogs Allowed On Broadwalk".

It means as if there are bicycle-riding dogs. There should be a full-stop after "Bicycle-riding". Thus:

"No Bicycle Riding. Dogs Allowed On broadwalk".

9. Fat Kids For Sale

This is a sign near a goat farm in Philadelphia. Since "Kid" is very often used for children, one would think that children are being sold there. The sign should be:

"Fat Goat Kids For Sale".

10. All Skirts One Half Off

This is a silly sign in Appleton. It means that the shop-keeper is removing half of your pants. He actually means that he is selling them at half the price. The sign should be:

"Prices of All Skirts One and a Half Down".

11. Shop At White Line When Red

This is a sign on the Connecticut River Bridge, East Haddam. This is just silly. "Red" means angry. The sign should be:

"Stop At White Line When the Signal Is Red".

12. Parking For Kings Only

This is a sign on the King's super-market in Plainfield, New Jersey. This is silly. It should be:

"Parking For Kings' Market Only".

13. Everything For Men Over 77 Years

This is a silly sign over Perlink's in Canton, Missouri. It should be:

"Everything For Men. Over 77 Years of Service".

14. No Trespassing By Owner

This means as if the owner is not allowed to trespass on his property. There should be a dash between "No Trespassing" and "By owner" and this should be given in two lines:

No Trespassing

—By Owner

54

Even this can cause confusion. So it should be:

No Trespassing
—*Order by Owner*

15. Nuts and Prunes Drive in

This is a sign on the Mountain View restaurant in California. It is wrong. It means as if nuts and prunes drive in the Mountain View. It should be:

"Nuts and Prunes. Drive in".

Just a fullstop will serve the purpose.

16. Proper Lady Excluded!

This is a sign in the West Coast dance hall. "The management reserves the right to exclude any lady it thinks proper".

Change the word "Proper" to "Improper".

17. Blind Man Driving!

This is a sign on the truck of a man dealing in window shades:—"A Blind Man Is Driving This Truck".

It should be:

"A Window Blindsman Is Driving This Truck".

18. Be Sure You Have Entered Before Leaving

This is a sign outside a warehouse. It is ludicrous. The owner means that you should enter your name in the register before leaving. It should be, "Be Sure You Have Registered Before Leaving".

19. You can Millions have

This is a sign on a rough Rocky Mountain—"Oh, Yes, You can, Millions Have". It does not make clear whether the millions have driven on this road and you can also drive; or millions have fallen down the mountain and you can also fall down if you are not careful. The right sign should have been:

"Oh Yes, You Can Drive. Millions Have Driven".

9

NOT WRONG—BUT LUDICROUS

Some business advertisements are not grammatically wrong but these are ludicrous, and so these are considerably worse than being wrong. To invite a joke at your own cost cannot be a matter of pleasure for a businessman. But some of the business people are so clever that they laugh at the cost of the customer or the visitor.

For example, study the following:

1. Proud & Brag

This name of a firm in Whitter, California is not good, because it is bad to be proud and even worse to brag. The firm should not have kept this name.

2. A Leak

This is the name of a plumber in Springfield, Illinois. This also is a bad name because a plumber's job is to plug the leak and not to create one!

3. Block & Clever

This is the name of a firm of meat-dealers in Kingston, Canada. The Name is appropriate.

4. Burnham & Overbake

This is the name of a bakery in Newark, New Jersey. The name is not good. A bakery should neither burn ham nor overbake things.

5. Doolittle & Bumm

This is the name of a firm of lawyers in German town, U.S.A. This is not a good name. "Bumm" means a fool and "do-little" you know well. It appears as if the lawyers claim that they invite only fools as clients and promise to do little for them!

6. Steele & Keep

This is the name of a firm of property dealers in Seattle. The name is very bad. It shows they want their customers to steal properties and then keep them by law. Of course "Steele" and "Keep" are the names of partners. But the firm's name does need a change and is not happily chosen.

7. O'Neill and Pray

This is the name of a firm of manufacturers of church benches in Chicago. The name is suitable.

8. Sole

This is the name of a shoemaker in Brooklyn, N.Y. The name is good.

9. For Women Only

This is a sign in an aircraft-factory employing women.

"No Swearing—There May be Gentlemen Present". The word should have been 'Gentle People'.

10. Capacity

In an American hotel:

"Our Capacity is 76".
Don't Try to prove Yours !

This is ludicrous. It should have been:

"Accommodation Limited to 76 Only".

11. Repair Shop

This notice in a New York repair shop is quite good:

"We Fix Everything but Football Games".

12. Fix Everything Except Broken Hearts

The Indian advertisement of "Quickfix" serve better than the American.

"Fixes Everything except Broken Hearts".

13. To Warn Thieves

This notice in a Detroit restaurant is excellent:

"As our Silverware is not Medicine, it should not be Taken After Meals".

14. King of Notices

This advertisement in Miami, Florida, can be said to be the king of all kings of notices put up by the businessmen:

"There may be A Housing Shortage in Miami. But there is Plenty of Room in the Dade County Jail. Stay Out of This Patch"!

10

MISARRANGEMENT OF WORDS

Misarrangement of words can make a real nonsense of something quite sensible. For example, study the following:

1. Officer for Target

In the Green Bay, U.S.A., policemen going on duty noted a new entry in the day book.

"See the bulletin board for the list of officers to shoot for target practice".

It means as if officers are to be shot for target practice! Actually, officers are to practise target shooting. Therefore, the sentence ought to be:

"See on the bulletin board, to shoot for target practice, the list of officers".

2. Twenty-Four Hogs

A nervous young lawyer, counsel for a farmer in the accidental rail-road crossing death of twenty-four hogs, was trying to impress the jury with the magnitude of his client's loss. Said he:

"Twenty-four hogs! Think of it, gentlemen, twice the number there are in the jury box".

The lawyer meant no ill-will towards the jury. He should have said:

"Twenty-four hogs! Think of it, twice the number of gentlemen there are in the jury".

This is what he meant. Having used the word gentlemen once, he felt disinclined to repeat it. That created the error. If he wanted to use the word "gentlemen" only once, then he should have used them later than earlier.

3. The Character That Fishes

A Georgia Court ruled: "That fishing is not bad, that a man has not a bad character that fishes".

It should be: "That fishing is not bad, that a man that fishes has not a bad character".

4. Fair, Fat and Fifty

One judge in Massachusetts had this say on ruling:

"The correspondent is fair, fat and fifty. The first she admits, the second she cannot deny and the third, she does".

The last is ambiguous. It should be: "Third, she denies".

11

NEWSPAPER KNAVERIES

Give me any newspaper of the world on any day of the year, and I will show you that it contains spelling, grammatical, and meaning mistakes, not only in the internal pages but on the front page itself.

Intentional or International?

This is a front page News Item dated Washington, May 2, 19... (U.P.I.) and is more a mistake of the United Press of India than of the *Hindustan Times* which copied it verbatim on the front page of its issue dated May 3, 19..., Column 6, and carried the news to the back page from the front page on Column 5.

The title of the news is *"Nixon Offer Does not Satisfy Panel"*. The American Parliament told House Judiciary Committee that his offer of transcripts instead of tapes failed to comply with its subpoena.

"We have found, quite candidly, that these transcripts are not accurate", Mr. Doar said, "I'm not suggesting any international distortions".

The word intended, and probably spoken, by the lawyer Johan M. Doar, could not be INTERNATIONAL. The lawyers are very careful about the use of their words: It is no doubt the mistake of the Press Agency, from which the *Hindustan Times* made a hasty copy.

In newspaper offices the people don't have time to think. They leave all the thinking to the readers.

2. Excess or Access?

"Iran is expected to provide credit in access of one billion dollars to India to help *maxmize the capcity off its eksport-orented industeries*".

Access—excess

Maxmize—maximize

Capcity—capacity

Off—of

Eksport—export

Orented—Oriented

Industeries—Industries.

3. Plain or Plane
"Another violation by Pak *plain*."

It should be "plane".

4. Rite or Right?

"President Venkataraman offered flowers and performed a *right* where Nehru was cremated".

The word should be "rite".

5. Heartiest or Heart-felt

"Mr. Chou En-lai conveyed *heartiest* condolence to Mrs. Indira Gandhi on the death of Shri Jawaharlal Nehru".

The word should be "heart-felt".

6. Heart-felt or Heartiest?

"Mr. Chou En-lai has conveyed his 'heart-felt' thanks to Mrs. Gandhi and the government of India for their support to the resolution on China's admission to the United Nations and the Taiwan expulsion".

The word should be "heartiest".

7. Upheld or Help Up?

"The Supreme Court today reaffirmed and *help up* the right of minorities whether based on religion or language, to establish and administer educational institutions of their choice".

The word should be "Upheld".

8. Canceled or Cancelled?

"The Railway Board went a *head* and *canceled* many *tranes* today".

"A head" should be one combined word "Ahead".

Canceled—Cancelled

Tranes—Trains.

9. Fuel or Feul

"Mr. Madhu Limaye stated in *Look Saba twoday* when *alged* that the INA Khukri *was sank* by the Pakistanis because of the inferior *feul-suplied* by the Indian Oil Corporation".

Look Saba—Lok Sabha

Twoday—today

Alged—alleged

Was sank—was sunk

Feul—fuel

Suplied—supplied.

10. Diary or Dairy?

"The Minister made a note in his *dairy*".

The word should be "diary".

11. Dairy or Diary?

"The increase of *diary* products will create a revolution in the country".

The word should be "dairy".

12. Pact or Packet?

"The Golan Heights packet is yet uncertain....."

The word should be "pact".

13. Packet or Pact?

He brought me a pact of cigarettes.

the word should be "packet".

14. Peace or Piece?

The United Nations is lending the best of its energies towards *piece* efforts.

The word should be "peace".

15. Here or Hear?

The U.S. Secretary of State, Dr. Henry Kissinger, said *hear* today......

The word is "here".

16. Workers or Warkers?

"PM *diplores* sectional *approch of warkers.....*"

Diplores—deplores

Approch—approach

Warkers—workers

17. City Whether?

It should be "City Weather".

18. Whether India?

It should be "Whither India".

19. Wholesale or Wholesail?

The "wholesail" price index has gone up.

It should be "wholesale"

20. Aid or Aide

"India wants ADB aide for members....."

The word should be "aid".

21. Aide or Aid?

"He is an aid to the President......"

The word should be "aide".

22. Curfue or Curfew

"125 *arested* for *peeple's curfue....*"

Arested—arrested

Peeple—people

Curfue—curfew.

23. Due or Dew?

"The labourers received their *dew* today".

The word should be "due".

24. Dew or Due?

"Due fell on the grass in the cold night".

The word should be "Dew".

25. Robed or Robbed?

"Cinema cashier was *robed* last night".

The word should be "robbed".

26. Robbed or Robed?

"The Pope was *robbed* in the scarlet".

The word should be "robed".

---

27. Fares or Fairs

"The Railway Ministry decided to increase the *fairs....*"

The word should be "fares".

28. Advise or Advice?

"The government was *adviced* to take immediate steps".

The word should be "advised".

29. Van or Vain?

"*Detension* was *qustioned* in the bank *robery vain* case".

Detension—detention

Qustioned—questioned

Robery—robbery

Vain—Van.

30. Rezident or Resident?

"The Janakpuri *rezident* was arrested".

The word should be "Resident".

31. Addit or Audit?

"We have not yet received the *addit* report".

The word should be "Audit".

32. Lacksity or Laxity?

"*Lacksity* in Delhi hospitals assailed...."

The word should be "laxity".

33. Steal or Steel?

"Anxiety over fall in *steal* production ...."

The word should be "steel".

34. Relected or Re-elected?

"Mr. Godey Murahari was today unanimously *relected* Deputy Chairman of Rajya Sabha...."

The word should be "re-elected".

35. Homage or Homeage?

"The Lok Sabha paid *homeage* to Dr. Ramdhari Singh Dinkar...."

The word should be "homage".

12

PROPER USE
OF PROPER NOUNS

A Proper Noun denotes one particular person or thing as distinct from every other, such as, Bhagat Singh, New Delhi, India, etc.

The writing of a Proper Noun should always begin with a capital letter. A word or phrase is added sometimes to prevent ambiguity of reference. Thus, we say:

Bhagat Singh of Azad Market.

Shahid Bhagat Singh

Sant Bhagat Singh

Bhagat Singh Bajaj

Harnam Singh Bhagat Singh

This helps us to distinguish different persons with the same name.

A Proper Noun is said to be used as a Common Noun when it denotes some rank or office, some class or persons or things. Such words as comparison of one great man with another carry articles as Common Nouns, even though they are Proper Nouns.

Jawaharlal was the Julius Caesar of India.

Khan Abdul Gaffar Khan was the Gandhi of the Frontier.

Delhi is the Paris of India.

1. I met peter yesterday. ☒
   I met Peter yesterday. ☑

2. Kashmir is Switzerland of India. ☒
   Kashmir is the Switzerland of India. ☑

3. I have met queen Elizabeth. ☒
   I have met Queen Elizabeth. ☑

4. Have you seen prime minister? ☒
   Have you seen the Prime Minister? ☑

5. I went to the New Delhi. ☒
   I went to New Delhi. ☑

6. I have lived in a Mumbai. ☒
   I have lived in Mumbai. ☑

7. My mother died at Mumbai. ☒
   My mother died in Mumbai. ☑

8. My father lived in Calcutta. ☒
   My father lived at Calcutta. ☑

   (*Rule*: 'In' is used for a big place; "at" is used for a small place).

9. Chennai is to south of India. ☒
   Chennai is in the south in India. ☑

10. Colombo is in the south of India. ☒
    Colombo is to the south of India. ☑

11. Many roberts and peters were present there. ☒
    Many Roberts and Peters were present there. ☑

12. I met a John on the road. ☒
    I met John on the road. ☑

13. This firm is called the Ram, Sham & Co. ☒
    This firm is called Ram, Sham & Co. ☑

14. This is the office of the Messrs. Ram, Shyam & Co. ☒
    This is the office of Messrs. Ram, Shyam & Co. ☑

15. Have you met M/s. Good Brothers? ☒
    Have you been to M/s. Good Brothers? ☑

16. Have you been to Taj Mahal? ☒
    Have you been to the Taj Mahal? ☑

17. I took my bath in Jamuna. ☒
    I took my bath in the Jamuna. ☑

18. How long have you lived in the Simla? ☒
    How long have you lived in Simla? ☑

19. Sri Lanka is in Indian Ocean. ☒
    Sri Lanka is in the Indian Ocean. ☑

20. My brother has gone to Punjab. ☒
    My brother has gone to the Punjab. ☑

21. This is the Missouri of USA, not Mussoorie of India. ☒
    This is Missouri of USA, not Mussoorie of India. ☑

22. This is Cochin of India, not Cochin of China. ☒
    This is Cochin of India, not the Cochin of China. ☑

23. Nepoleon was the Julius Çaesar. ☒
    Nepoleon was a Julius Caesar. ☑

24. Napoleon was Julius Caesar of France. ☒
    Napoleon was the Julius Caesar of France. ☑

25. Congress is not the ruling party of India. ☒
    The Congress is not the ruling party of India. ☑

26. I went to Congress House. ☒
    I went to the Congress House. ☑

27. This is a firm of the Birla Brothers. ☒
    This is a firm of Birla Brothers. ☑

28. These are M/s. Birla Brothers. ☒
    This is M/s. Birla Brothers. ☑

29. Have you read song celestial? ☒
    Have you read the Song Celestial? ☑

30. Alexander the great king of Macedonia, was the conqueror of the India. ☒
    Alexander the Great, King of Macedonia, was the conqueror of India. ☑

31. George was a king. ☒
    George was king. ☑

32. I met the king George. ☒
    I met King George. ☑

33. Czar of Russia was lord of Europe. ☒
    The Czar of Russia was the lord of Europe. ☑

34. I am Hindu.
    I am a Hindu.

35. Arjuna was bravest of Pandavas. ☒
    Arjuna was the bravest of the Pandavas. ☑

36. A Daniel was the Jewish prophet. ☒
    Daniel was a Jewish prophet. ☑

13

COMPOUND
CORRECTIVES

The use of compound words is gaining ground in all languages all over the world.

It is necessary that these compound words should be carefully studied and properly used.

Some of the compound words with their wrong and right use are given below:

1. She is a hearted chicken girl. ☒
   She is a chicken-hearted girl. ☑

2. He died heart-broken. ☒
   He died broken-hearted. ☑

3. This is an addle-head minister. ☒
   This is an addle-headed minister. ☑

4. This is a crusted gold chandelier. ☒
   This is a gold-crusted chandelier. ☑

5. The patriot was a man hearted lion. ☒
    The patriot was a lion-hearted man. ☑

6. You are a do nothing. ☒
    You are a do-nothinger. ☑

7. I want a pen headed diamond. ☒
    I want a diamond-headed pen. ☑

8. He is make sunshine boy. ☒
    He is a make-hay-while-the-sun-shines boy. ☑

9. You are a man devil may care. ☒
    You are a devil-may-care man. ☑

10. It was a will phenomenon of the wisp. ☒
    It was a will-o'-the wisp phenomenon. ☑

11. From today this is a bridge tomorrow. ☒
    This is a from-today-to-tomorrow bridge. ☑

12. He failed not with standing his efforts. ☒
    He failed his efforts notwithstanding. ☑

13. I am please call me what you. ☒
    I am call-me-what-you-please man. ☑

14. He is a barking enemy dog seldom bite. ☒
    He is a barking-dog-seldom-bite enemy. ☑

15. He is a man do not put off till tomorrow what you can do today.   ☒

He is a do-not-put-off-till-tomorrow-what-you-can-do-today man.   ☑

16. Oscar Wilde is a man do not put off till tomorrow what you can do the day after.   ☒

Oscar Wilde is a do-not-put-off-till-tomorrow-what-you-can-do-the-day-after man.   ☑

14

THE GENUINE USE
OF GENDERS

Most of the people do not know the genuine use of gender. They often become confused between masculine and feminine genders. They have seldom a right idea of common and neuter genders.

1. This woman is a bachelor. ☒
    This woman is a spinster. ☑

2. We caught a bear with five cubs. ☒
    We caught a sow with five cubs. ☑

3. I want a he-dove for a pet. ☒
    I want a buck for a pet. ☑

4. This colt will make a good mare. ☒
    This colt will make a good horse. ☑

5. Will this filly make a good horse? ☒
    Will this filly make a good mare? ☑

6. This is a she-dog. ☒
   This is a bitch. ☑

7. This duck gives no eggs. It is a male. ☒
   This drake gives no eggs. It is a male. ☑

8. This man is a bee. ☒
   This man is a drone. ☑

9. He is a nun. ☒
   He is a monk. ☑

10. This is a he-goose. ☒
    This is a gander. ☑

11. I want a male and female horse. ☒
    I want a horse and a mare. ☑

12. This is a male fish. ☒
    This is a milter. ☑

13. This is a female fish. ☒
    This is a spawner. ☑

14. My nephew is a beautiful girl. ☒
    My niece is a beautiful girl. ☑

15. Sir, Lady, I cannot do this work. ☒
    Madam, I cannot do this work. ☑

16. The swain has five young ones. ☒
    The nymph has five young ones. ☑

17. My auntie is a wizard. ☒
    My auntie is a witch. ☑

18. I want a he-goat and a she-goat. ☒
    I want a billy-goat and a nanny-goat. ☑

19. Give me a he-sparrow and a she-sparrow. ☒
    Give me a cock-sparrow and a
    hen-sparrow. ☑

20. He-ass gives no milk. ☒
    Jack-ass gives no milk. ☑

21. I am forced to keep a male maid-servant. ☒
    I am forced to keep a man-servant. ☑

22. The landlord of this house is a woman. ☒
    The landlady of this house is a woman. ☑

23. She was the chairman of the meeting. ☒
    She was chairperson of the meeting. ☑

24. He is my servant-maid. ☒
    He is my man servant. ☑

25. She is our washerman. ☒
    She is our washerwoman. ☑

26. She is the author of this book. ☒
    She is the authoress of this book. ☑

27. This woman is a giant. ☒
    This woman is a giantess. ☑

28. She was our host. ☒
    She was our hostess. ☑

29. I want a lady peacock. ☒
    I want a peahen. ☑

30. Indira is patron of this club. ☒
    Indira is patroness of this club. ☑

31. Sarojini Naidu was a poet. ☒
    Sarojini Naidu was a poetess. ☑

32. She is my benefactor. ☒
    She is my benefactress. ☑

33. She is a conductor. ☒
    She is a conductress. ☑

34. This Negro is a beautiful woman. ☒

This Negress is a beautiful woman. ☑

35. She was a traitor to our plans. ☒
    She was a traitress to our plans. ☑

36. He is now a widow. ☒
    He is now a widower. ☑

37. She is a murderer. ☒
    She is a murderess. ☑

38. She is a headmaster. ☒
    She is a headmistress. ☑

39. This lady is a good administrator. ☒
    This woman is a good administrix. ☑

40. She is a beau. ☒
    She is a belle. ☑

41. Is your mother the executor of this deed? ☒
    Is your mother the executrix of this deed? ☑

42. Indira is an orphaness. ☒
    Indira is a girl orphan. ☑

43. This is an elephantess. ☒
    This is a she-elephant. ☑

44. Are you the manageress here? ☒
    Are you the manager here? ☑

15

PROVERBIATICS

The correct use of proverbs is as necessary as that of any other parts of speech.

Much wisdom of all times and climes lies in proverbs and it is unfortunate that modern generation is forgetting proverbs and their right usages.

Here are some proverbs within common knowledge, yet likely to be commonly misused.

1. Diamonds cut diamonds. ☒
   Diamond cuts diamond. ☑

2. A rolling stone gather no moss. ☒
   A rolling stone gathers no moss. ☑

3. A barking dog seldom kisses. ☒
   A barking dog seldom bites. ☑

4. Familiarity breads similarity. ☒
   Familiarity breeds contempt. ☑

5. There is no use catching the spilt milk. ☒
   There is no use crying over the spilt milk. ☑

6. As you so, sow shall you reep. ☒
   As you sow, so shall you reap. ☑

7. As a father, so a son. ☒
   Such a father, such a son. ☑

8. Do not sweep horses middle of the stream. ☒
   Do not swap horses mid stream. ☑

9. A bird in hands is worth too in the buses. ☒
   A bird in hand is worth two in the bush. ☑

10. Evil always came from good. ☒
    Good always comes out of evil. ☑

11. So you think as you become. ☒
    As you think, so you become. ☑

12. Life is not made of roses. ☒
    Life is not a bed of roses. ☑

13. Birds of feathers flocks togethers. ☒
    Birds of a feather flock together. ☑

14. Blood is fatter than water. ☒
    Blood is thicker than water. ☑

15. Blood far blood. ☒
    Blood for blood. ☑

16. No a man bye the company she keeps. ☒
    Know a man by the company he keeps. ☑

17. Do not put on until tomorrow what you
    work yesterday. ☒
    Do not put off till tomorrow what you can
    do today. ☑

16

PACKING KNACK
NUMBER KNAVERIES

Singular and plural seem to be the easiest form of grammar gadgets; but in these also some people are likely to make mistakes through sheer force of habit or ignorance. Just examine the following:

1. Guiding people is the part of a policeman's duties. ☒

   Guiding people is a part of a policeman's duty. ☑

2. Cat has many lifes. ☒

   Cat has many lives. ☑

3. A horse has hoofs. ☒

   A horse has hooves. ☑

4. Rooves must be repaired before the rains. ☒

   Roofs must be repaired before the rains. ☑

5. He brought me five scarfs. ☒
   He brought me five scarves. ☑

6. Five dwarves came to my house. ☒
   Five dwarfs came to my house. ☑

7. The kitchen is full of mouses. ☒
   The kitchen is full of mice. ☑

8. He owns many house. ☒
   He owns many houses. ☑

9. He has two father-in-laws. ☒
   He has two fathers-in-law. ☑

10. The Officer has two feet-men. ☒
    The Officer has two foot-men. ☑

11. They are knight-errants. ☒
    They are knights-errant. ☑

12. He has two steps-daughter. ☒
    He has two step-daughters. ☑

13. The Commander-in-chiefs of India and Pakistan have a hot telephone. ☒

The Commanders-in-chief of India and Pakistan have a hot telephone. ☑

14. The only agenda was salary for the watchman. ☒

The only agendum was salary of the watchman. ☑

15. Everything in war is a data of war. ☒
Every thing in war is a datum of war. ☑

16. This is an ova of the silkworm. ☒
This is an ovum of the silkworm. ☑

17. He submitted a memorandum to the minister. ☒

He submitted memoranda to the minister. ☑

18. Money and power are political medium. ☒
Money and power are political media. ☑

19. Show me the radiuses of these circles. ☒
Show me the radii of these circles. ☑

20. The letter has two appendixes. ☒
The letter has two appendices. ☑

21. I am an alumni of the Punjab University. ☒
I am an alumnus of the Punjab University. ☑

22. Money and power are focus of politics. ☒
    Money and power are focii of politics. ☑

23. Where are the axis of the sun and the moon? ☒
    Where are the axes of the sun and the moon? ☑

24. This is the first serie of my novel. ☒
    This is the first series of my novel. ☑

25. How many apparatuses you have here? ☒
    How many apparatus have you here? ☑

26. This is the analysis of two sentences. ☒
    These are the analyses of two sentences. ☑

27. The terminus of Central and Western Railways are in Mumbai. ☒
    The terminii of Central and Western Railways are in Mumbai. ☑

28. What are the basis of your report? ☒
    What is the basis of your report? ☑

29. India is passing through many crisis. ☒
    India is passing through many crises. ☑

30. Your hypothesis are not correct. ☒
    Your hypothesis is not correct. ☑

31. They have submitted two thesis for doctorate. ☒

They have submitted two theses for doctorate. ☑

32. Sunrise is a great phenomena. ☒

Sunrise is a great phenomenon. ☑

33. What is the criterion of justice and fairplay? ☒

What are the criteria of justice and fairplay? ☑

34. You must approach the information bureau of embassies for this. ☒

You must approach the information bureaux of embassies for this. ☑

35. Monsieur Ram and Sham were present. ☒

Messieurs Ram and Sham were present. ☑

36. How many madams were there? ☒

How many mesdames were there? ☑

37. This cattle is mine. ☒

These cattle are mine. ☑

38. This vermin does much harm. ☒

These vermin do much harm. ☑

39. Every minister is a swine. ☒

The ministers are all swine. ☑

40. The people has all the power. ☒
    The people have all the power. ☑

41. The people of the world must unite. ☒
    The peoples of the world must unite. ☑

42. He gave me many abuses. ☒
    He gave me much abuse. ☑

43. Please give me all these informations. ☒
    Please give me all this information. ☑

44. The child knows all the alphabets. ☒
    The child knows all the alphabet. ☑

45. The house is full of furnitures. ☒
    The house is full of furniture. ☑

46. I have two offsprings. ☒
    I have two offspring. ☑

47. He writes many poetries. ☒
    He writes poems. ☑

48. These fields have lovely sceneries. ☒
    These fields have lovely scenery. ☑

49. The old folk is dead. ☒
    The old folk are dead. ☑

50. I have five deers. ☒
    I have five deer. ☑

51. How many sheeps have you? ☒
    How many sheep have you? ☑

52. I have nine braces of birds. ☒
    I have nine brace of birds. ☑

53. The farmer has five yokes of oxen. ☒
    The farmer has five yoke of oxen. ☑

54. He weighs ten stones and a half. ☒
    He weighs ten stone and a half. ☑

55. That box weighs three hundred weights. ☒
    That box weighs three hundred weight. ☑

56. I have only three pices. ☒
    I have only three pice. ☑

57. Please lend me a ten-dollars note. ☒
    Please lend me a ten dollar note. ☑

58. This is twelve-months story. ☒
    This is a twelve-month story. ☑

59. I want a three-feet rule. ☒
    I want a three-foot rule. ☑

60. This is an eight-days clock. ☒
    This is an eight-day clock. ☑

61. This is a six-years-old child. ☒
    This is a six year-old child. ☑

62. I have forty heads of cattle. ☒
    I have forty head of cattle. ☑

63. Hindus and Muslims are brothers. ☒
    Hindus and Muslims are brethren. ☑

64. Please put on your cloths. ☒
    Please put on your clothes. ☑

65. He gave five clothes to the tailor. ☒
    He gave five cloths to the tailor. ☑

66. Sheila and Swarna are genii of the class. ☒
    Sheila and Swarna are geniuses of the class. ☑

67. How many indices has this book? ☒
    How many indexes has this book? ☑

68. They put the flags on the staffs. ☒
    They put the flags on the staves. ☑

69. The staves of the army were present. ☒
    The staffs of the army were present. ☑

70. He gave me many advice. ☒
    He gave me much advice. ☑

71. The army force was used. ☒
    The army forces were used. ☑

72. Please give me my spectacle. ☒
    Please give me my spectacles. ☑

73. Please vacate my premise. ☒
    Please vacate my premises. ☑

74. I want new pant. ☒
    I want new pants. ☑

75. I got a summon for court. ☒
    I got a summons for court. ☑

76. He asked me for an alm. ☒
    He asked me for alms. ☑

77. These are my riches. ☒
    This is my riches. ☑

17

TRICKY-TRACKY ADJECTIVES

It is easy to use most of the adjectives but some of them are very tricky.

1. He did not give me some money. ☒
   He did not give me any money. ☑

2. Any men die young. ☒
   Some men die young. ☑

3. Many a man are poor. ☒
   Many a man is poor. ☑

4. Few men are millionaires. ☒
   A few men are millionaires. ☑

5. A sundry men went away. ☒
   Sundry men went away. ☑

6. Any twenty men were present. ☒
   Some twenty men were present. ☑

7. A several men came. ☒
   Several men came. ☑

8. He had little bread. ☒
   He had a little bread. ☑

9. He had a much bread. ☒
   He had much bread. ☑

10. I have an enough milk. ☒
    I have enough milk. ☑

11. Have you had some bread? ☒
    Have you had any bread? ☑

12. I had many loaf of breads. ☒
    I had many loaves of bread. ☑

13. Few loaves will fill the stomach. ☒
    A few loaves will fill the stomach. ☑

14. Did you bring some pens? ☒
    Did you bring any pens? ☑

15. She ate a apple. ☒
    She ate an apple. ☑

16. He is a heir. ☒
    He is an heir. ☑

17. Will you spend a hour with me? ☒
    Will you spend an hour with me? ☑

18. Lal Bahadur Shastri was a honest man. ☒
    Lal Bahadur Shastri was an honest man. ☑

19. The ten women had every a gun. ☒
    Each of the ten women had a gun. ☑

20. Milk is an useful drink. ☒
    Milk is a useful drink. ☑

21. Metre is an unit. ☒
    Metre is a unit. ☑

22. This is an one-eyed giant. ☒
    This is a one-eyed giant. ☑

23. This is an history book. ☒
    This is a history book. ☑

24. 15th August is a historical day. ☒
    15th August is an historical day. ☑

25. He came each four hours. ☒
    He came every four hours. ☑

26. He was down with fever each other day. ☒
    He was down with fever every other day. ☑

27. You can take each side. ☒
    You can take either side. ☑

28. Which book is that? ☒
    What book is that? ☑

29. What book do you like best? ☒
    Which book do you like the best? ☑

30. He is an asleep man. ☒
    He is a man asleep. ☑

31. He went by the train down. ☒
    He went by the down train. ☑

32. This is a chair to sit. ☒
    This is a chair to sit on. ☑

33. This is to drink water. ☒
    This water is to drink. ☑

34. This book is the smallest than all. ☒
    This book is the smallest of all. ☑

35. The fast you go, the quick you reach. ☒
    The faster you go, the quicker you reach. ☑

36. This chair is bad than that. ☒
    This chair is worse than that. ☑

37. He is my older brother. ☒
    He is my elder brother. ☑

38. Please read farther. ☒
    Please read further. ☑

39. I went further from home. ☒
    I went farther from home. ☑

40. You are superior than me. ☒
    You are superior to me. ☑

41. This cloth is inferior than that. ☒
    This cloth is inferior to that. ☑

42. You are junior than me. ☒
    You are junior to me. ☑

18

PRICKY PRONOUNS

Pronouns are not very difficult to handle but some of them can be really pricky.

A Pronoun is a word used instead of a noun or noun-equivalent.

We use pronouns to make writing less cumbersome. For example, consider the following:

"Ram saw a snake in the garden, this snake Ram thought would hurt Ram, unless Ram killed the snake with a stick, Ram had in his hand".

This sentence would be expressed as:

"Ram saw a snake in the garden, which he thought would hurt him unless he killed it with a stick which he had in his hand".

1. This house is my. ☒
   This house is mine. ☑

2. This is mine house. ☒
   This is my house. ☑

3. My pen and your are without ink. ☒
   My pen and yours are without ink. ☑

4. This horse of you is tired. ☒
   This horse of yours is tired. ☑

5. I took he's book. ☒
   I took his book. ☑

6. This book is he. ☒
   This book is his. ☑

7. Look through mine eyes with thine. ☒
   Look through my eyes with thine. ☑

8. Look through mine eyes. ☒
   Look through my eyes. ☑

9. I hid mine. ☒
   I hid myself. ☑

10. We hid ours. ☒
    We hid ourselves. ☑

11. The children seated. ☒
    The children seated themselves. ☑

12. The children sat themselves. ☒
    The children sat. ☑

13. We us saw the thief. ☒

We ourselves saw the thief. ☑

14. The walls them fell. ☒
    The walls themselves fell. ☑

15. Your pen is black; my is yellow. ☒
    Your pen is black; mine is yellow. ☑

16. My pen is black; your is yellow. ☒
    My pen is black; yours is yellow. ☑

17. My sister came yesterday; we were glad
    to see she. ☒
    My sister came yesterday; we were glad
    to see her. ☑

18. This pen is her. ☒
    This pen is hers. ☑

19. This is hers pen. ☒
    This is her pen. ☑

20. The boys fell asleep as soon as them
    arrived. ☒
    The boys fell asleep as soon as they
    arrived. ☑

21. Its sad to hear bad news. ☒
    It's sad to hear bad news. ☑

22. It is probable that it will rain today. ☒
    It is probable that it may rain today. ☑

23. Work and play are both necessary to health, this gives you rest and that gives you energy. ☒

Work and play are both necessary for health; this gives you rest and that gives you energy. ☑

24. I love dogs but not cats; these are faithful but these are not. ☒

I love dogs but not cats; these are faithful but those are not. ☑

25. The air of hills is cooler than plains. ☒

The air of hills is cooler than that of plains. ☑

26. The houses of Defence Colony are larger than Rajouri Gardens. ☒

The houses of Defence Colony are larger than those of Rajouri Gardens. ☑

27. I studied English when I was young and in Lahore. ☒

I studied English when I was young and at Lahore. ☑

28. There are four bright boys and three dull in our class. ☒

There are four bright boys and three dull ones in our class. ☑

29. Rich men are not happier than the poor. ☒

The rich men are not happier than the poor ones. ☑

30. A stranger cannot be received twice in the same house. ☒

A stranger cannot be received twice as such in the house. ☑

31. None but the brave deserve the fair. ☒
None but the brave deserves the fair. ☑

—*Dryden*

32. I cannot tell you now that what has happened. ☒

I cannot tell you now what has happened. ☑

33. The laws are that the judge says they are. ☒
The laws are what the judge says they are. ☑

34. Who breaks this law will be punished. ☒
Whoever breaks this law will be punished. ☑

35. This is not a good book I expect. ☒
    This is not such a good book as I expected. ☑

36. This is the same man came yesterday. ☒
    This is the same man that came yesterday. ☑

37. There was no one present saw the dead. ☒
    There was no one present but saw the dead. ☑

19

VERBS THAT WORRY

A verb is a word for saying something about some person or thing. Most of the verbs are simple but sometimes their use can worry the user.

1. Fetch me back that book. ☒
   Fetch me that book. ☑

2. Go, fetch that book. ☒
   Go, bring that book. ☑

   "Fetch" means to go and bring.

3. We envy him for his good luck. ☒
   We envy him his good luck. ☑

4. I forgive you for your faults. ☒
   I forgive you your faults. ☑

5. I taught English to him. ☒
   I taught him English. ☑

6. Do not refuse to me the small loan. ☒
   Do not refuse me the small loan. ☑

7. Lend to me ten rupees. ☒
   Lend me ten rupees. ☑

8. We gave a prize to the girl. ☒
   We gave the girl a prize. ☑

9. They fined on me ten rupees. ☒
   They fined me ten rupees. ☑

10. You owe to me five rupees. ☒
    You owe me five rupees. ☑

11. Please show to me the way. ☒
    Please show me the way. ☑

12. Please tell to me the story. ☒
    Please tell me the story. ☑

13. He played a trick on me. ☒
    He played me a trick. ☑

14. You saved me from much trouble. ☒
    You saved me from trouble. ☑

15. He sold his pen to me. ☒
    He sold me his pen. ☑

16. He was come over by the enemy. ☒
    He was overcome by the enemy. ☑

17. The river flowed over its banks. ☒
    The river overflowed its banks. ☑

18. He sat himself down. ☒
    He seated himself. ☑

    He sat down.

19. The stone is feeling rough. ☒
    The stone feels rough. ☑

20. Honey is tasted sweet. ☒
    Honey tastes sweet. ☑

21. The house does not let. ☒
    The house is not to let. ☑

22. The house is building. ☒
    The house is being built. ☑

23. The house is finished. ☒
    The house is being finished. ☑

24. The book is printing. ☒
    The book is being printed. ☑

25. The cows are milking. ☒
    The cows are being milked. ☑

26. The hotel was three years building. ☒
    The hotel was three years under building. ☑

27. We shall go equal. ☒
    We shall go equals. ☑

28. You had not good remain here. ☒
    You had better not remain here. ☑

29. Ran he not? ☒
    Did he not run? ☑

30. Wrote he? ☒
    Did he write? ☑

31. You not yet finished reading this letter? ☒
    Have you not yet finished reading this letter? ☑

32. Murder unless it has no tongue will speak. ☒
    Murder though it has no tongue will speak. ☑

33. Man though he has no tongue to speak. ☒
    Man unless he has no tongue will speak. ☑

34. You need not to send those books to me. ☒
    You need not send those books to me. ☑

35. You dare not to say this. ☒
    You dare not say this. ☑

36. He made me to come home early. ☒
    He made me come home early. ☑

37. I watched you to come and to go.   ☒
    I watched you come and go.   ☑

38. I have not known him to laugh for
    nothing.   ☒
    I have not known him laugh for nothing.   ☑

39. He ordered me go.   ☒
    He ordered me to go.   ☑

40. I was not permitted go.   ☒
    I was not permitted to go.   ☑

41. Good be with the dead.   ☒
    Better be with the dead.   ☑

42. I had taken this than that.   ☒
    I had rather taken this than that.   ☑

43. I had run than walk.   ☒
    I had sooner run than walk.   ☑

44. A rabbit is able to run than walk.   ☒
    A rabbit is better able to run than walk.   ☑

45. The joker did nothing but laughing.   ☒
    The joker did nothing but laugh.   ☑

46. Err is human; forgive divine.   ☒
    To err is human; to forgive divine.   ☑

47. I am–tell the truth–quite tired of this work. ☒

I am–to tell you the truth–quite tired of this work. ☑

48. They were unstruck–so speak–on hearing the news of Shastri's death. ☒

They were thunderstruck–so to speak–on hearing the news of Shastri's death. ☑

49. I am tired with work. ☒
I am tired of work. ☑

50. Shot the tiger, he returned home. ☒
Having shot the tiger, he returned home. ☑

51. He is teaching Hindi his son. ☒
He is teaching his son Hindi. ☑

52. Having taught English he is a good scholar. ☒

Having been taught English, he is a good scholar. ☑

53. We saw him to fight a hard battle. ☒
    We saw him fight a hard battle. ☑

54. He began to eat to sit down. ☒
    Having sat down, he began to eat. ☑

55. This praised much man was a rogue. ☒
    This much-praised man was a rogue. ☑

56. Gold is a dug out of earth metal. ☒
    Gold is a metal dug out of earth. ☑

57. This is the rose faded. ☒
    This is the faded rose. ☑

58. He is a candidate failed. ☒
    He is the failed candidate. ☑

59. He is a soldier returned. ☒
    He is the returned soldier. ☑

60. He took over the car from right. ☒
    He overtook the car from right. ☑

61. This is a horse dead. ☒
    This is a dead horse. ☑

62. This a flower withered. ☒
    This is a withered flower. ☑

63. Indira is the sun risen. ☒
    Indira is the risen sun. ☑

64. Here is the guest departed. ☒
    Here is the departed guest. ☑

65. The elephant of Nehru, proceeded to England, is for sale. ☒
    The elephant of Nehru, which has proceeded to England, is for sale. ☑

66. There is no scent in the rose faded this morning. ☒
    There is no scent in the faded rose this morning. ☑

67. I am sorry for the candidate failed in the last examination. ☒
    I am sorry for the candidate who failed in the last examination. ☑

68. He is Daniel come to judgment. ☒
    He is a Daniel come to judgment. ☒

69. He came to my house in past times. ☒
    He came to my house in times past. ☑

70. He is a decended man from the royal family. ☒
    He is a man descended from the royal family. ☑

71. You are a man well read. ☒
    You are a well read man. ☑

72. He is a boy behaved well. ☒
    He is well-behaved boy. ☑

73. You are a man spoken out. ☒
    You are an outspoken man. ☑

74. You are a boy of retired nature. ☒
    You are a boy of retiring nature. ☑

75. This is an evil heart man. ☒
    This is an evil-hearted man. ☑

76. This is a hot-head girl. ☒
    This is a hot-headed girl. ☑

77. This is a red-colour rose. ☒
    This is a red-coloured rose. ☑

78. This youth is faced rough. ☒
    This is a rough-faced youth. ☑

79. This is a book paged many. ☒
    This is a many-paged book. ☑

80. This is a snake hooded. ☒
    This is a hooded snake. ☑

81. This is a long monkey armed. ☒
    This is a long-armed monkey. ☑

82. This is a wooded hill thickly. ☒

This is a thickly-wooded hill. ☑

83. You are a man minded noble. ☒
You are a noble-minded man. ☑

84. Man is an animal blooded warm. ☒
Man is a warm-blooded animal. ☑

85. Walk along the street I met a friend. ☒
Walking along the street I met a friend. ☑

86. Met my friend, I went away. ☒
Having met my friend, I went away. ☑

87. He sat down, tired toil. ☒
He sat down toil-tired. ☑

Being tired with toil, he sat down.

88. You made a mistake admitting what you say. ☒
Admitting what you say, you made a mistake. ☑

89. Goodness gone still returns. ☒
Goodness being gone still returns. ☑

90. Turn to the left, you will find my house. ☒
Turning to the left, you will find my house. ☑

91. Sleep to life is necessary. ☒
Sleep is necessary for life. ☑

92. He is clever in teaching English. ☒
    He is clever at teaching English. ☑

93. He is pleased being taught English. ☒
    He is pleased at being taught English. ☑

94. He is proud having fought in war. ☒
    He is proud of having fought in war. ☑

95. This was a work my doing. ☒
    This was a work of my doing. ☑

96. This set me think. ☒
    This set me thinking. ☑

97. The wall fell; I am vexed at having fallen. ☒
    The wall fell; I am vexed at its having fallen. ☑

98. I depend on the wall built immediately. ☒
    I depend on the wall being built immediately. ☑

99. I am engaged in reading careful of this book. ☒

I am engaged in the careful reading of this book. ☑

100. I am pleased at my surroundings. ☒

I am pleased with my surroundings. ☑

101. I went away along all my belongings. ☒

I went away along with all my belongings. ☑

102. Was I in your place, I would pay the rupee. ☒

Were I in your place, I would pay the rupee. ☑

103. You need not to send these books to me. ☒

You need not send these books to me. ☑

104. He was much pleased found a friend. ☒

He was much pleased having found a friend. ☑

105. The ship rose from the sea. ☒

The ship arose from the sea. ☑

106. The woman bore a children. ☒

The woman bore a child. ☑

107. I have forgot what you said. ☒

I have forgotten what you said. ☑

108. I have forsook the house. ☒
     I have forsaken the house. ☑

109. He has slew the truth. ☒
     He has slain the truth. ☑

110. The child slide down the wall. ☒
     The child slid down the wall. ☑

111. She was smote with pain. ☒
     She was smitten with pain. ☑

20

MAZES OF PHRASES

Phrases make a flowery language and phrases are known as flowers of language, but phrases are tricky things and if you are not careful and have not learnt your phrases carefully, you may fall in a phrasy-mazy language.

Phrases are more often likely to be used wrongly than rightly.

The correct usage of some common phrases is given below:

1. The boy fell in love head on heels. ☒
   The boy fell in love head over heels. ☑

2. Do not play duck and drake with your money. ☒
   Do not play ducks and drakes with your money. ☑

3. You passed in life with fire and water. ☒
   You passed in life through fire and water. ☑

4. People collect money with hook or with crook. ☒

   People collect money by hook or by crook. ☑

5. I do not know how to keep the wolf from my doors. ☒

   I do not know how to keep the wolf away from my door. ☑

6. He threw oil on the troubled water. ☒

   He threw oil on the troubled waters. ☑

7. It goes against your grains. ☒

   It goes against your grain. ☑

8. Take this news with grains of salt. ☒

   Take this news with a grain of salt. ☑

9. Do not put fuel on the fire. ☒

   Do not add fuel to the fire. ☑

10. Take the bull with the horns. ☒

    Take the bull by the horns. ☑

11. Take heart with grace. ☒

    Take heart of grace. ☑

12. The thief was caught red hand. ☒

    The thief was caught red handed. ☑

13. What is being cooked here? ☒

    What is cooking up here? ☑

14. You have a serpent in your sleeve. ☒
    You have a serpent up your sleeve. ☑

15. Please read the letter between each line. ☒
    Please read the letter between the lines. ☑

16. Please turn over the new pages of your life. ☒
    Please turn over the new page. ☑

17. Butt me no butts. ☒
    But me no buts. ☑

18. Your reputation has reached on the ground. ☒
    Your reputation has touched the ground. ☑

19. He earns pennies with the sweat of his brow. ☒
    He earns a penny by the sweat of his brow. ☑

20. Let us swim and sink together. ☒
    Let us swim or sink together. ☑

21. Let us make a friend. ☒
    Let us make friends. ☑

22. Do not let the grass dry under your feet. ☒
    Do not let the grass grow under your feet. ☑

23. You are of colour today. ☒
    You are off colour today. ☑

24. You are burning the candles at both ends. ☒
    You are burning the candle at both ends. ☑

25. Why destroy the midnight oil? ☒
    Why burn the midnight oil? ☑

26. You have taken the hearts out of your
    friends. ☒
    You have taken the heart out of your
    friends. ☑

27. When you are angry, bring the roofs
    down. ☒
    When you are angry, don't bring down the
    roof. ☑

28. Let us break breads and be friends. ☒
    Let us break bread and be friends. ☑

29. Let us do and die. ☒
    Let us do or die. ☑

30. Let us go half. ☒
    Let us go halves. ☑

31. When you cannot pay rent, take to
    moonlight flying. ☒
    When you cannot pay rent, take to
    moonlight flitting. ☑

32. The enemy took to their heals. ☒
    The enemy took to its heel. ☑

33. It makes my mouth watered. ☒
    It makes my mouth water. ☑

34. Let us change sword into ploughshare. ☒
    Let us turn swords into ploughshares. ☑

35. A practical man swims with the tides. ☒
    A practical man swims with the tide. ☑

36. I am between the devils and deeps. ☒
    I am between the devil and the deep. ☑

37. You are between the fire. ☒
    You are between two fires. ☑

38. Life is not a plot of roses. ☒
    Life is not a bed of roses. ☑

39. Don't push against the thorns. ☒
    Don't kick against the thorns. ☑

40. There are no points of honours in duels. ☒
    There is no point of honour in a duel. ☑

41. You must stand upon point. ☒
    You must stand upon points. ☑

42. She moved heavens and earths to get the job. ☒

   She moved heaven and earth to get the job. ☑

43. Victory is apples of discord. ☒

   Victory is an apple of discord. ☑

44. Let us bury the hatchets. ☒

   Let us bury the hatchet. ☑

45. Do not build a castle on air. ☒

   Do not build castles in the air. ☑

21

ADVERBS GOING AWRY

An Adverb is a word used to qualify any part of speech except a noun or pronoun. It is a word used to qualify a verb, adjective or other adverbs.

Angus and Bain admit that qualifying power of adverbs cannot be limited to adverbs. Marson points out that an adverb "sometimes modifies a preposition".

1. The bird flew exactly the child's headover. ☒
    The bird flew exactly over the child's head. ☑

2. I was sitting outside the door almost. ☒
    I was sitting almost outside the door. ☑

3. I wish to know how it happened precisely. ☒
   I want to know how precisely it happened. ☑

4. They locked the door before the thieves came shortly. ☒
   They locked the door shortly before the thieves came. ☑

5. The watch was found after it was lost long. ☒
   The watch was found long after it was lost. ☑

6. He arrived at midnight after a few hours. ☒
   He arrived a few hours after midnight. ☑

7. Evident that you were much distressed. ☒
   It was evident that you were much distressed. ☑

8. He is an almost drunkard. ☒
   He is almost a drunkard. ☑

9. I am sincerely your. ☒
   I am sincerely yours. ☑

10. I had met late Prime Minister Nehru. ☒
    I had met the late Prime Minister Nehru. ☑

11. The above account is wrong. ☒
    The account above is wrong. ☑

12. This is a mail up. ☒

This is an up mail. ☑

13. I live in a country far. ☒

I live in a far country. ☑

14. He is the cleverest man in the class almost. ☒

He is almost the cleverest man in the class. ☑

15. This is we live. ☒

This is where we live. ☑

16. Much men have, more they want. ☒

The more men have, the more they want. ☑

17. Soon you go, the good. ☒

The sooner you go, the better. ☑

18. I worked harder, because the teacher encouraged me. ☒

I worked the harder, because the teacher encouraged me. ☑

19. He came to my house latest. ☒

He came to my house last. ☑

20. This is the last model. ☒

This is the latest model. ☑

21. He fared badly than before. ☒
    He fared worse than before. ☑

22. He did it wiselier than you. ☒
    He did it more wisely than you. ☑

23. He long stayed with me. ☒
    He stayed with me long. ☑

24. He spoke loud. ☒
    He spoke aloud.
    He spoke loudly. ☑

25. He was little tired. ☒
    He was a little tired. ☑

26. You have enough slept. ☒
    You have slept enough. ☑

27. He went to the shop in where he found
    a snake. ☒
    He went to the shop wherein he found
    a snake. ☑

28. He comes to me sometime. ☒
    He comes to me sometimes. ☑

29. He stays with me sometimes. ☒
    He stays with me some time. ☑

30. I met him particular. ☒
    I met him in particular. ☑

31. We can do some work present. ☒
    We can do some work at present.
    We can do some work presently. ☑

32. The dog was set large. ☒
    The dog was set at large. ☑

33. Why are you going backward and forward? ☒
    Why are you going backwards and forwards? ☑

34. He comes to me of and on. ☒
    He comes to me off and on. ☑

35. We will meet bye and by. ☒
    We will meet by and by. ☑

36. By the bye, how is your mother? ☒
    By the by, how is your mother? ☑

37. The crop will come well. ☒
    The crop will come out well. ☑

38. Cholera has broken here. ☒
    Cholera has broken out here. ☑

39. No profits will come. ☒
    No profits will come in. ☑

40. He set on his journey. ☒
    He set out on his journey. ☑

41. Please do not put of this work. ☒
    Please do not put off this work. ☑

42. Plants are shooting. ☒
    Plants are shooting out. ☑

43. The Harijan was cast. ☒
    The Harijan was cast out. ☑

44. This house is to let out. ☒
    This house is to let. ☑

45. You are entire wrong. ☒
    You are entirely wrong. ☑

46. The patient will be good soon. ☒
    The patient will be well soon. ☑

47. He met through the door. ☒
    He met me half through the door. ☑

48. These books are sold over one rupee each. ☒
    These books are sold at over one rupee each. ☑

49. The bargain is of. ☒
    The bargain is off. ☑

50. You are well of. ☒
    You are well off. ☑

51. I put my hand over the table. ☒
    I put my hand on the table. ☑

52. The bear is live. ☒
    The bear is alive.
    This is a live bear. ☑

53. He has come beyond the seas. ☒
    He has come from beyond the seas. ☑

54. I bought this under half its value. ☒
    I bought this at under half its value. ☑

55. From the garden the dog ran in the house. ☒
    From the garden the dog ran into the house. ☑

56. The flag is flying onto the house. ☒
    The flag is flying on the house. ☑

57. The house stands over the bank. ☒
    The house stands over against the bank. ☑

58. I came cross a friend. ☒
    I came across a friend. ☑

59. I live among the trees. [X]
    I live amongst the trees. [✓]

60. We live besides the stream. [X]
    We live beside the stream. [✓]

61. Beside this pencil I have a pen. [X]
    Besides this pencil I have a pen. [✓]

62. Consider your age you have done well. [X]
    Considering your age you have done well. [✓]

63. Crops have been spoiled owing to rains. [X]
    Crops have been spoiled owning to the rains. [✓]

64. All saves one left. [X]
    All save one left. [✓]

65. Despite of his riches he is not happy. [X]
    Despite his riches he is not happy. [✓]

66. In spite his riches he is not happy. [X]
    In spite of his riches he is not happy. [✓]

67. Wheat sells at one kilo for a rupee. [X]
    Wheat sells at one kilo a rupee. [✓]

68. He comes once in a week. [X]
    He comes once a week. [✓]

69. She suffers more than me. ☒
    She suffers more than I. ☑

70. I will not take ten rupees than less. ☒
    I will not take less than ten rupees. ☑

71. He got more than he asked. ☒
    He got more than he asked for. ☑

72. All but comes daily. ☒
    All but one come daily. ☑

73. He was but all ruined. ☒
    He was all but ruined. ☑

74. I cry for your help. ☒
    I cry for you to help. ☑

75. He lives in front my house. ☒
    He lives in front of my house. ☑

76. Me he works in opposition. ☒
    He works in opposition to me. ☑

77. He walked going in car instead. ☒
    He walked instead of going in a car. ☑

78. With reference your letter, please come. ☒
    With reference to your letter, please
    come. ☑

22

CONJUNCTIONS THAT COAX

A Conjunction is a word for joining and for no other purpose. It never qualifies a word. It simply joins words and sentences.

1. The rain fell we reached home before. ☒
   We reached home before the rain fell. ☑

2. I got prize and you got a job. ☒
   I got a prize and you got a job. ☑

3. He was degraded both and expelled. ☒
   He was both degraded and expelled. ☑

4. He is also guilty and you. ☒
   He is guilty, and you also. ☑

5. You are an idler and careless to. ☒
   You are an idler and careless too. ☑

6. He as well as you are guilty. ☒
   He as well as you is guilty. ☑

7. You as well as he is guilty. ☒
   You as well as he are guilty. ☑

8. He no less than you are guilty. ☒
   He no less than you is guilty. ☑

9. You no less than he is guilty. ☒
   You no less than he are guilty. ☑

10. He was not only accused but convicted. ☒
    He was not only accused but also convicted. ☑

11. Either this man nor you stole my purse. ☒
    Either this man or you stole my purse. ☑

12. Neither you or he is a thief. ☒
    Neither you nor he is a thief. ☑

13. Neither you nor he or I was present there. ☒
    Neither you nor he nor I was present there. ☑

14. Either you, I or he did this work. ☒
    Either you or he or I did this work. ☑

15. Leave this room, you will be fined. ☒
    Leave this room or you will be fined. ☑

16. Work hard; or you will fail. ☒
    Work hard; otherwise you will fail. ☑

17. I am sad and hopeful. ☒
    I am sad but hopeful. ☑

18. He is rich and not happy. ☒
    He is rich and yet not happy. ☑

19. All men were against him; he succeeded. ☒
    All men were against him; nevertheless,
    he succeeded. ☑

20. He failed; he stuck to his work. ☒
    He failed, however, he stuck to his work. ☑

21. Wise men work as where fools shun it. ☒
    Wise men work whereas fools shun it. ☑

22. I will die far all men are mortal. ☒
    I will die for all men are mortal. ☑

23. Go where you like; not stay here. ☒
    Go where you like; only do not stay here. ☑

24. He was found guilty and he was hanged. ☒
    He was found guilty and therefore, he
    was hanged. ☑
    He was found guilty and so he was
    hanged.

25. It is time to go; let us start. ☒
It is time to go; so let us start. ☑

26. He is as clever as me. ☒
He is as clever as I. ☑

27. He likes you no less than I. ☒
He likes you no less than me (he likes me). ☑

28. The sea is as deep as the mountains. ☒
The sea is as deep as mountains are high. ☑

29. He is wiser than better. ☒
He is wiser than good. ☑

30. He wished to know if I was ready to help him. ☒
He wished to know if I were ready to help him. ☑

31. Ten o'clock is the hours we start. ☒
Ten o'clock is the hour when we start. ☑

32. Tell me the reason you left us. ☒
Tell me the reason why you left us.
Tell me why you left us. ☑

33. Tell me the reason which you left us. ☒
    Tell me the reason for which you left us. ☑

34. This the house which we first lived. ☒
    This is the house in which we first lived.
    ·This is the house wherein we first lived. ☑

23

IDIOMATIC INCORRECTIONS

Idioms are quite often wrong used by those who do not care to understand them properly and have no proper grasp of their implications. They are simple constructions with deep meaning and so hasty reader or writer finds in them a pitfall in which he slips unknowingly.

Here are a few idioms likely to be misused:

1. Who will dispose off this property?   ☒
   Who will dispose of this property?   ☑

2. The boy was cut of in the bloom of his life.   ☒
   The boy was cut off in the bloom of his life.   ☑

3. Please keep your words.   ☒
   Please keep your word.   ☑

4. Who is carrying your business? ☒
   Who is carrying on your business? ☑

5. You have fallen in bad company. ☒
   You have fallen in with bad company. ☑

6. They worked hand with hand. ☒
   They worked hand in hand. ☑

7. Two and two make four. ☒
   Two and two makes four. ☑

8. She looks on my house. ☒
   She looks after my house. ☑

9. He looks like his father. ☒
   He looks after his father. ☑

10. He is calling you a bad name. ☒
    He is calling you bad names. ☑

11. You can put on here for two days. ☒
    You can put up here for two days. ☑

12. Plague carried many men. ☒
    Plague carried off many men. ☑

13. You have much work on hand. ☒
    You have much work in hand. ☑

14. You have much time in hand. ☒
    You have much time on hand. ☑

15. The king put the prisoner in death. ☒
    The king put the prisoner to death. ☑

16. You are cold on you wife. ☒
    You are cold to your wife. ☑

17. The boy was plucked up in the examination. ☒
    The boy was plucked in the examination. ☑

18. The old man went in life bravely. ☒
    The old man went through life bravely. ☑

19. Don't be hard too boys. ☒
    Don't be hard to boys. ☑

20. The plan has not yet got of the ground. ☒
    The plan has not yet got off the ground. ☑

21. He set every thing to naught. ☒
    He set everything at naught. ☑

22. You are not playing fairly. ☒
    You are not playing fair. ☑

23. The thief was sentenced for imprisonment. ☒
    The thief was sentenced to imprisonment. ☑

24. My hand is full. ☒
    My hands are full. ☑

25. Where are you putting in? ☒
    Where are you putting at? ☑

26. Please call me no name. ☒
    Please call me no names. ☑

27. What are you driving to? ☒
    What are you driving at? ☑

28. Please run into the book. ☒
    Please run through the book. ☑

29. The man died with poverty. ☒
    The man died of poverty. ☑

30. The boy is good far nothing. ☒
    The boy is good for nothing. ☑

31. Please carry to the next page. ☒
    Please carry over to the next page. ☑

32. You cannot rely in him. ☒
    You cannot rely on him. ☑

33. You are of colour today. ☒
    You are off colour today. ☑

34. A politician should have feel on the people. ☒

A politician should have felt of the people. ☑

35. They fell over the thief. ☒
They fell on the thief. ☑

36. Hit on the target. ☒
Hit at the target. ☑

37. You have fallen off grace. ☒
You have fallen from grace. ☑

38. Pluck flower is prohibited. ☒
Plucking flowers is prohibited. ☑

39. You are sitting on the chair. ☒
You are sitting in the chair. ☑

40. They carried war for two years. ☒
They carried on war for two years. ☑

41. Light has gone off. ☒
Light has gone out. ☑

42. Summer has set. ☒
    Summer has set in. ☑

43. Cement has set up. ☒
    Cement has set. ☑

44. We set his home in London. ☒
    We set up his home in London. ☑

45. She died heart broken. ☒
    She died broken-hearted. ☑

46. The pencil has broken in two. ☒
    The pencil has broken into two. ☑

47. This is a way with the world. ☒
    This is a way of the world. ☑

48. The king carried of the day. ☒
    The king carried off the day. ☑

49. Don't fly at range. ☒
    Don't fly into range. ☑

24

INKED IN INTERJECTIONS

An interjection is merely an exclamatory sound thrown in a sentence to denote some strong feeling or emotion.

There are some standard forms of interjection mistakes which should be carefully noted.

1. Think she should have died! ☒
   To think that she should have died. ☑

2. Wish that I had gained that horse! ☒
   Would that I gained that horse! ☑

3. Whether I could see him once more! ☒
   If I could see him once more! ☑

4. Hale, all hale! ☒
   Hail! All hail! ☑

5. Lack a day ! ☒
   Alack a day! ☑

6. Goodby! ☒
   Goodbye! ☑

7. Fairwell! ☒
   Farewell! ☑

8. Fee! fee! ☒
   Fie! File! ☑

9. Hallow! ☒
   Hello! ☑

10. Shaw! ☒
    Pshaw! ☑

11. Woe me! ☒
    Woe is me! ☑

12. Was I there to help you! ☒
    Were I there to help you! ☑

13. Brave! ☒
    Bravo! ☑

14. Cheer! ☒
    Cheerio! ☑

15. O.K. ☒
    All correct! ☑

25

MISTAKES OF MISQUOTATIONS

Vedas, Bible, Koran, other scriptures and writings of great men and sayings and proverbs are quite often misquoted, sometimes deliberately to create a desired effect; but quite often through lack of proper knowledge.

There is the story of a young man, a college student, who was travelling from Cambridge to Oxford, in the days of the good old horse carriages, and he quoted something which he said was from Shelley. Close by was sitting a Professor, who took out complete works of Shelley from his pocket and asked the boy to find out where the quotation was. The boy failed to find the necessary quotation and said, "Oh, I think the quotation is from Keats". Next the professor took out complete works of Keats from his pocket and asked him to locate the quotation. The youngster failed again and said, "I remember, it is from Byron". The Professor gave him works of Byron also. The boy was non-plussed and jumped out of the carriage, saying, "He has got the whole library in his pocket".

Those kinds of Professors are no more alive today, the people who carried libraries in their pockets. So, misquotation is carried on, on a large scale with vengance. Sometimes misquotation is deliberate for the sake of effect. For example:

Shakespeare's lines:

Sigh no more, ladies, sigh no more,

Men are deceivers ever;

One foot on sea and one on shore,"

To one place constant never.

This may be quoted as:

'Sign no more, Indira, sigh no more,

Politicians are deceivers, ever;

One foot in Janata and one in Congress,

To one party constant never."

This is harmless misquotation, but there are mischievous misquotations to subserve certain purpose on the principle, "A devil may quote the Bible for his purpose". For example, during the war of elections in March 1977, ex-Prime Minister Indira Gandhi was reported to have said: "It was on the advice of the Congress President, D.K. Borooah that Sanjay Gandhi joined the Youth Congress to revitalize the organization". The next day Mr. Borooah was reported to have denied that he had ever advised Sanjay

Gandhi to join the Youth Congress. The next day Mr. Borooah was reported to have denied his denial. Thus, Indira and Borooah added darkness to ignorance without shedding any light.

Here are some common quotations which are frequently misused:

1. Man purpose, God disposes. ☒
   Man proposes, God disposes. ☑

2. "Do not put of till tomorrow what you can do the day after". ☒
   Do not put off till tomorrow what you can do today. ☑

3. Eat, drink and be merry, because tomorrow ye diet. ☒
   Eat, drink and be merry, because tomorrow we die. ☑

4. Empty vessel has no voice. ☒
   Empty vessel makes much noise. ☑

5. There is no use carrying over spilt milk. ☒
   There is no use crying over spilt milk. ☑

6. The days of your life are membered. ☒
   The days of your life are numbered. ☑

7. There is a destiny that sharpens our bends, Rough-how them how you will. ☒

There's destiny that shapes our bends,
Rough how them how you will. ☑

(Shakespeare)

8. If winter came, can spring be for behind? ☒

   If winter comes, can spring be far behind? ☑

   (Shelley)

9. Beauty's truth, truth's beauty, that is all.
   You know and you should know. ☒

   Beauty is truth, truth beauty—that's all.
   Ye know and ye need to know. ☑

   (Keats)

10. As children to flies, we are to gods,
    They kill us for their entertainment. ☒

    As flies to children, we are to gods,
    They kill us for their sport. ☑

    (Shakespeare)

11. It is virtue to have a joint's strength,
    But tyranny to abuse it like a joint. ☒

    'Tis virtuous to a giant's strength,
    But tyrannous to use it like a giant. ☑

    (Shakespeare)

12. Too bee or not too bee,
    that is the song. ☒

    To be or not to be,
    that is the question. ☑

    (Shakespeare)

13. Capitalism is heaven compared to Socialism, but hell compared to Feudalism. ☒

Capitalism is hell compared to Socialism but heaven compared to Feudalism. ☑

(*V.I. Lenin*)

14. Men should stop fighting insects and start fighting the lions. ☒

Men should stop fighting among themselves and start fighting insects. ☑

(*Luther Burbank*)

15. All governments are, of course, for liberty. ☒

All government, of course, is against liberty. ☑

(*H.L. Mencken*)

16. The governing of trade has all ways been monopolized by the most literate and the most rascal individuals of mankind. ☒

The trade of governing has always been monopolized by the most ignorant and the most rascally individuals of mankind. ☑

(*Thomas Paine*)

26

DIFFERENT DIALOGUE
DIFFICULTIES

1. Take rest before going some further.
   Take rest before going any further.

2. Did you bring some book?
   Did you bring any book?

3. Take some book you like.
   Take any book you like.

4. He is not so good he looks.
   He is not so good as he looks.

5. He is not a fool as he looks. ☒
   He is not such a fool as he looks. ☑

6. He is trembled as he stood. ☒
   He trembled as he stood. ☑

7. Your is not the same book as my. ☒
   Your is not the same book as mine. ☑

8. Hot as the sun is, we must go out. ☒
   Hot though the sun is, we must got out.
   Although the sun is hot, we must go out. ☑

9. I condemn you a judge. ☒
   I condemn you as a judge. ☑

10. As regards this man, we can decide
    nothing. ☒
    Regarding this man, we can decide
    nothing. ☑

11. My pen is better one than your. ☒
    My pen is a better one that yours. ☑

12. You are working good today. ☒
    You are working well today. ☑

13. Do you despise your better? ☒
    Do you despise your betters? ☑

14. The men have both arrived. ☒
    Both the men have arrived. ☑

15. You are a knave and fool both. ☒
    You are both a knave and a fool. ☑

16. Who could have but you done this? ☒
    Who could have done this but you? ☑

17. You are a man of qualities, not honest. ☒
    You are a man of qualities, but not
    honest. ☑

18. Each of the two is ruined. ☒
    Either of the two is ruined. ☑

19. We could find you but no one. ☒
    We could find you but no one else. ☑

20. He is neither a fool nor knave. ☒
    He is neither a fool nor a knave. ☑

21. He is weak nor poor. ☒
    He is weak but not poor. ☑

22. He has a real trouble; he could not have
    wept. ☒
    He has real trouble, else he would have
    not wept. ☑

23. You have enough eaten food. ☒
    You have eaten enough food.
    You have eaten food enough. ☑

24. He was dead half with fear. ☒
    He was half dead with fear. ☑

25. There was no one absent without the teacher. ☒
    There was no one absent but the teacher. ☑

26. Perdition catch my soul, I do love you. ☒
    Perdition catch my soul but I do love you. ☑

27. He is ruined in each case. ☒
    He is ruined in either case. ☑

28. Little food will kill your hunger. ☒
    A little food will kill your hunger. ☑

29. The dying man has eaten a little. ☒
    The dying man has eaten little. ☑

30. Let us wait here little. ☒
    Let us wait here a little. ☑

31. He eats bread than butter. ☒
    He eats more bread than butter.
    He eats bread rather than butter. ☑

32. More was done than is expected. ☒
    More is done than was expected. ☑

33. More men came then went. ☒
    More men came than went. ☑

34. I saw him more. ☒
    I saw of him more. ☑

35. I do not agree with each side. ☒
    I agree with neither side. ☑

36. Neither you or I can do it. ☒
    Neither you nor I can do it. ☑

37. Stand by what I speak to you. ☒
    Stand by when I speak to you. ☑

38. He is my bye relative. ☒
    He is my near relative. ☑

39. He must need go. ☒
    He must needs go. ☑

40. One is apt to waste his time. ☒
    One is apt to waste one's time. ☑

41. My horse is a black. ☒
    My horse is a black one. ☑

42. The rupee I had was stolen. ☒
    The only rupee I had was stolen. ☑

43. Do what you like: keep silence only. ☒
    Do what you like: only keep silence. ☑

44. A square thing does not fit in a round hole. ☒

A square thing does not fit into a round hole. ☑

45. Draw a circle round a centre. ☒

Draw a circle around a centre. ☑

46. The flies are flying around and around. ☒

The flies are flying round and round. ☑

47. I have not seen you for Monday last. ☒

I have not seen you since Monday last. ☑

48. It has been raining since four days. ☒

It has been raining for four days. ☑

49. I took this house four weeks since. ☒

I took this house four weeks ago. ☑

50. You are not a man as I expected. ☒

You are not such a man as I expected. ☑

51. He came to me on such day. ☒

He came to me on such a day. ☑

52. You are a coward; I am not that. ☒
    You are a coward; I am not such. ☑

53. The light of the sun is brighter than the moon. ☒
    The light of the sun is brighter than that of the moon. ☑

54. These are students whom I have never seen more honest. ☒
    These are students more honest than whom I have never seen. ☑

55. He was fond of any drink than wine. ☒
    He was fond of any drink other than wine. ☑

56. He was better than he is now. ☒
    He was better then than he is now. ☑

57. I see, will not help me then. ☒
    I see, then, you will not help me. ☑

58. The ass is a dull animal. ☒
    Ass is a dull animal. ☑

59. I am going to Punjab. ☒
    I am going to the Punjab. ☑

60. I am going to the Simla ☒
    I am going to Simla. ☑

61. The much, the merry. ☒
    The more, the merrier. ☑

62. He worked harder to stand first. ☒
    He worked the harder to stand first. ☑

63. He is too fond of play. ☒
    He is very fond of play. ☑

64. We to must expect to die. ☒
    We too must expect to die. ☑

27

PUNCTUATION PIN-PRICKS

Punctuation is not considered very important now-a-days but sometimes it can be very prickly and gore a sentence to death and murder.

1. We should live slowly sweetly soberly all the time. ☒

   We should live slowly, sweetly, soberly all the time. ☑

2. Friends Romans countrymen lend me your ears. ☒

   Friends, Romans, countrymen, lend me your ears. ☑

3. He hoped then that he would be pardoned. ☒

   He hoped, then, that he would be pardoned. ☑

4. As Caesar loved me I weep for him as he was fortunate I rejoice at it as he was

valiant I honour him but as he was ambitious I slew him as there is a tear for his love joy for his fortunate honour for his valour and death for his ambition. ☒

As Caesar loved me, I weep for him; as he was fortunate, I rejoice at it; as he was valiant, I honour him; but as he was ambitious, I slew him. So there is tears for his love; joy for his fortune; honour for his valour; and death for his ambition. ☑

5. Nonsense, how can you talk such a rubbish. ☒

Nonsense! How can you talk such a rubbish. ☑

6. The soldiers said death before honour. ☒

The soldier said, "Death before honour". ☑

7. Wine is a mocker said the wise king. ☒

"Wine is a mocker", said the wise king. ☑

8. Honble chief justice. ☒

The Hon'ble Chief Justice. ☑

9. Land ahead shouted the crew. ☒

   "Land ahead"! shouted the crew. ☑

10. Here lies the great false marble where. ☒

    There lies the great false marble where? ☑

11. At the age of ten such is the power of
    genius he could read and write. ☒

    At the age of ten, such is the power of
    genius, he could read and write.

    At the age of ten—such is the power of
    genius—he could read and write. ☑

28

PERKY PREPOSITIONS

Nothing is perkier in English language than the use of prepositions. The word may be the same but it requires a different preposition for every different purpose. And sometimes the use of any preposition makes the sentence wrong!

1. He ordered for cook's dismissal. ☒
   He ordered the cook's dismissal. ☑

2. You do not obey to my orders. ☒
   You do not obey my orders. ☑

3. This girl resembles to my sister. ☒
   This girl resembles my sister. ☑

4. I will inform to your mother. ☒
   I will inform your mother. ☑

5. He recommended for you to the minister. ☒
   He recommended you to the minister. ☑

6. This book has benefited to me much. ☒
   This book has benefited me much. ☑

7. Have you disposed the application? ☒
   Have you disposed of the application? ☑

8. The doctor will combat with the disease. ☒
   The doctor will combat disease. ☑

9. I confess some suspicion of your work. ☒
   I confess to some suspicion of your work. ☑

10. You must compensate this loss to me. ☒
    You must compensate me for this loss. ☑

11. Please carefully investigate into the case. ☒
    Please investigate the case carefully. ☑

12. Do not boast your success. ☒
    Do not boast of your success. ☑

13. Do not violate against the rules. ☒
    Do not violate the rules. ☑

14. Do not sign on the contract. ☒
    Do not sign the contract. ☑

15. He dispensed my services. ☒
    He dispensed with my services. ☑

16. I could not prevail him to do this. ☒
    I could not prevail upon him to do this. ☑

17. Please assist to me in this matter. ☒
Please assist me in this matter. ☑

18. He will not listen your request. ☒
He will not listen to your request. ☑

19. You must apply the Rationing Officer for food. ☒
You must apply to the Rationing Officer for food. ☑

20. Ten prizes were competed. ☒
Ten prizes were competed for. ☑

21. You cannot depend his word. ☒
You cannot depend on his word. ☑

22. He complained upon you. ☒
He complained against you. ☑

23. Do not be angry upon me. ☒
Do not be angry with me. ☑

24. He does not admit any friendship. ☒
He does not admit of any friendship. ☑

25. He meditated on a murder. ☒
He meditated a murder. ☑

26. Please partake a meal. ☒
Please partake of a meal. ☑

27. Do not muse your losses. ☒
    Do not muse on your losses. ☑

28. That thought pervades through my whole mind. ☒
    That thought pervades my whole mind. ☑

29. You are right to hold that opinion. ☒
    You are right in holding that opinion. ☑

30. You are not fit to manage for this house. ☒
    You are not fit to manage this house. ☑

31. Do not discourage him to learn English. ☒
    Do not discourage him against learning English. ☑

32. I have a passion for studying. ☒
    I have a passion to study. ☑

33. Repent to have been idle. ☒
    Repent of having been idle. ☑

34. Do not despair to succeed. ☒
    Do not despair of succeeding. ☑

35. Do not hinder me to do this. ☒
    Do not hinder me from doing this. ☑

36. I am intent to win. ☒
    I am intent on winning. ☑

37. You are confident of win. ☒
    You are confident of winning. ☑

38. Do not resign yourself to fail. ☒
    Do not resign yourself to failure. ☑

39. I am debarred to help you. ☒
    I am debarred from helping you. ☑

40. Abstain to speak evil of others. ☒
    Abstain from speaking evil of others. ☑

41. I insist on you to go. ☒
    I insist on your going. ☑

42. Do not prevent me to work. ☒
    Do not prevent me from working. ☑

43. Do not check me to borrow money. ☒
    Do not check me from borrowing money. ☑

44. Refrain to do evil. ☒
    Refrain from doing evil. ☑

45. Insist to have your fee paid. ☒
    Insist on having your fee paid. ☑

46. Persist to do this. ☒
    Persist in doing this. ☑

47. Do not accuse me with theft. ☒

Do not accuse me of theft. ☑

48. Work in accordance to rule. ☒
    Work in accordance with rule. ☑

49. I did it according with your orders. ☒
    I did it according to your orders. ☑

50. You must accede with my request. ☒
    You must accede to my request. ☑

51. You have no ability to this work. ☒
    You have no ability for this work. ☑

52. She got an advantage on you. ☒
    She got an advantage over you. ☑

53. Do not take advantage over my mistake. ☒
    Do not take advantage of my mistake. ☑

54. There is no advantage for learning. ☒
    There is no advantage of learning. ☑

55. You cannot be admitted to this place. ☒
    You cannot be admitted into this place. ☑

56. I have no acquaintance to her. ☒
    I have no acquaintance with her. ☑

57. Do not battle to your luck. ☒
    Do not battle with your luck. ☑

58. I am ready to bargain with a pen. ☒
    I am ready to bargain for a pen. ☑

59. I cannot bargain to you. ☒
    I cannot bargain with you. ☑

60. I have no version to ugly men. ☒
    I have no aversion to ugly men. ☑

61. I have no authority on my wife. ☒
    I have no authority over my wife. ☑

62. He is an authority over English. ☒
    He is an authority on English. ☑

63. You must pay attention for your study. ☒
    You must pay attention to your study. ☑

64. I arrived in Delhi. ☒
    I arrived at Delhi. ☑

65. I arrived at India. ☒
    I arrived in India. ☑

66. There is no antidote for this. ☒
    There is no antidote to this. ☑

67. I have no aptitude to Maths. ☒
    I have no aptitude for Maths. ☑

68. I have no affinity for money. ☒
    I have no affinity with money. ☑

69. I have no contempt to anyone. ☒
    I have no contempt for anyone. ☑

70. Fashion is a cloak to vice. ☒
    Fashion is a cloak for vice. ☑

71. You must take care for my books. ☒
    You must take care of my books. ☑

72. He is a candidate to elections. ☒
    He is a candidate for elections. ☑

73. What is the cause for trouble? ☒
    What is the cause of trouble? ☑

74. What is the cause of anxiety? ☒
    What is the cause for anxiety? ☑

75. I have no desire of wealth. ☒
    I have no desire for wealth. ☑

76. Can you guess on the truth? ☒
    Can you guess at the truth? ☑

77. I have no duty for you. ☒
    I have no duty to you. ☑

78. You must glance on this book. ☒
    You must glance at this book. ☑

79. This is the failure in your plan. ☒
    This is the failure of your plan. ☑

80. We need economy for time. ☒
    We need economy of time. ☑

81. There is no drawback for your success. ☒
    There is no drawback to your success. ☑

82. You are a heir for this house. ☒
    You are an heir to this house. ☑

83. I have no hope for your success. ☒
    I have no hope of your success. ☑

84. I have no interest of this subject. ☒
    I have no interest in this subject. ☑

85. You have no nerve of riding. ☒
    You have no nerve for riding. ☑

86. I have no lust with money. ☒
    I have no lust for money. ☑

87. I have no need of assistance. ☒

I have no need for assistance. ☑

88. I am in need of your assistance. ☒
    I am in need for your assistance. ☑

89. You are a martyr for gout. ☒
    You are a martyr to gout. ☑

90. You are a martyr to freedom. ☒
    You are a martyr for freedom. ☑

91. This is a scene on the window. ☒
    This is a scene at the window. ☑

92. This is a scene from the sea. ☒
    This is a scene of the sea. ☑

93. I have preference to tea. ☒
    I have preference for tea. ☑

94. I have preference for tea on coffee. ☒
    I have preference for tea to coffee. ☑

95. He was annoyed with my work. ☒
    He was annoyed at my work. ☑

96. He was annoyed on the cook. ☒
    He was annoyed at the cook. ☑

97. You are accountable to this loss. ☒
    You are accountable for this loss. ☑

98. You are accountable for your boss. ☒
    You are accountable to your boss. ☑

99. He was anxious about his safety. ☒
    He was anxious for his safety. ☑

100. I am anxious for the result. ☒
     I am anxious about the result. ☑

101. I am concerned on this accident. ☒
     I am concerned about this accident. ☑

102. I am concerned about your health. ☒
     I am concerned for your health. ☑

103. I am concerned on this business. ☒
     I am concerned in this business. ☑

104. Do not be eager in distinction. ☒
     Do not be eager for distinction. ☑

105. He is eager for the pursuit of money. ☒
     He is eager in the pursuit of money. ☑

106. She is engaged with John. ☒
     She is engaged to John. ☑

107. I am engaged with business. ☒
    I am engaged in business. ☑

108. Do not be disappointed with success. ☒
    Do not be disappointed of success. ☑

109. Do not be disappointed of your good luck. ☒
    Do not be disappointed in your good luck. ☑

110. I am disappointed in you. ☒
    I am disappointed with you. ☑

29

COMMON ERRORS
IN LETTERS

People commit many common errors in everyday letters. Consequently, they fail to hit the mark. The other person whom you are trying to impress is depressed, and may refuse to do the work that you want him, expect him, and pray to him to do for you or help you do it. A single spelling or grammatical mistake may reveal the character of the writer of a correspondence and the other party may judge you from the single mistake and not the hundred and one good things that you have said.

Besides, a single mistake may lead to different meaning and distort your meaning and cause you huge damage. A lady stenographer typed out:

"Any more policies on the old rates will not be affected" when the boss wanted her to type:

"Any more policies on the old rates will not be effected".

Because of this one mistake the American Insurance company suffered a loss of 100,000 dollars before the mistake was discovered and rectified.

It is mostly in the nature of "fan mail." There are suggestions and cheers, a pat on the back, with an occasional letter of criticism and even "applications as candidates to contest elections".

The postman who does the round of the 7, Jantar Mantar Road (Janta Party headquarters) and 5, Rajendra Prasad Road (AICC head office) must be an unhappy man, not to speak of the one who brings the mail at Mrs. Gandhi's and Mr. Jagjivan Ram's residence. His burden is heavier than ever before and he has to make more rounds than possibly he did in the last five years.

To get an idea of how exactly the masses view the activities of the two parties and their stalwarts, we decided to go through a cross-section of what the postman brings in his bag.

They run into numerous closely-written pages in all languages—mostly Hindi and English—and by all sections of people from all parts of the country.

A lot of them make sense and others do not.

A sample from the latter group "Application for Congress Ticket for Election to Lok Sabha".

The "applicant" goes on to list amongst his qualifications, his "child-history" and the fact that he "always loved the Congress and wore (spelt as wearned) black cloth up to the independence days, attended birthday of Subhash Chandra Bose, listened to every speech of Nehru and attended the funeral ceremony of Mahatma Gandhi".

As a footnote, and an additional qualification, he adds that though his brother-in-law in Canada had invited him to stay there, he had refused and that he often wrote to Mrs. Indira Gandhi.

There is another "application" at the Congress office—wherein the "applicant" claims that his candidature should be seriously considered since he is the "only Indian who has washed his head in his guru's blood on 30-1-48 (the day Mahatma Gandhi was assassinated). He goes on to claim the support of the numerous elections of society in the area he lives in, on numerous grounds.

Surprisingly, the AICC office has quite a number of these "applications". The mail which comes in, is channelled through the four general secretaries. Apart from this, some mail from the Prime Minister's House, specially the one pertaining to organisational matters, is directed here. On an average, the office deals with about 300 letters everyday. Of them, a mere one tenth are replied.

The mail at 7, Jantar Mantar Road is more "fiery and spirited". A postcard from a young student pledges support to the party "though I cannot donate notes (my pocket-money is finished) or votes. I am still under-age, I assure you that I will assist you in making the people more enlightened and help you in making the burden of poverty on many lighter."

A school-teacher from Jind writes that since he is a Government employee and afraid of being harassed, he had come dressed as a sadhu to offer his services at the party office, but nobody could guide him to the right people and that he should be summoned by telegram.

Not that the supporters of the Congress are lacking. There are letters galore at the AICC office criticising the association of different groups within the Janata Party frame-work, "I feel immensely proud that you have exposed the sham of collective leadership" or "every right-thinking person must support more than ever before the dynamic leadership along with the policy and the programme of the Prime Minister".

At the Janata Party office, too, there are cheques and donations in response to advertisements in newspapers and glowing tributes—"it is not a donation, it is an ahuti (oblation)" or everywhere the wind is blowing in favour of the Janata Party or hailing it as the "dream party". There are also letters donating kidneys for "JP" and lottery tickets for the party campaign.

The largest number of letters, perhaps, are devoted to suggestions for campaign style. The "Janata Mail" at both centres, is full of letters from well-meaning supporters who point out again and again the need for popularising the party's symbol.

A party worker writes about questioning a villager whom he would vote for— "The Janata Party" came the reply. "What is the party's symbol", the workers asked. Pat came the reply "gai aur bachhra" (cow and calf).

Another letter-writer points out that most of the people do not understand the meaning of "haldhar" (ploughman) which symbolises the party.

On the Congress side, the suggestions include one for declaring every second and fourth Saturday if not every Saturday as a holiday in order to woo the Central Government employees. Another admirer suggests that since there had been a lot of criticism of family-planning measures and in order to "call the bluff of the Janata Party", the Health Minister should ask all cases of unmarried or involuntary sterilisation to be brought to light within seven days and steps should be taken to "reverse these sterilisations".

A short-film-maker suggests a small film and with a picture of two children followed by a voice announcing "follow the leader" (Mrs. Gandhi herself had two children) and a picturisation of the red triangle.

At both places, there are poems galore running into several pages. There are "opportunists"—letters from manufacturers of office equipment or publishing firms. At the AICC office there is a letter from the editor of a small newspaper in Himachal Pradesh, who points out that since he had been supporting the party for the past few years, the maximum number of advertisements should be given to his paper.

The "Grievance Column" runs long and cumbersome in the mail bag, which is dumped on the doorstep of both party offices. There are people who apparently think that this is the right time to get all grievances and complaints redressed.

Very seldom there is criticism. The AICC file surprisingly contains a letter which cynically suggests "Haji Mastan as a Congress Party nominee for the coming elections. He is a devout Muslim, a self-made man, he can spend more money than anybody else". But perhaps somebody filed it unknowingly in the "Suggestions Column".

The mail bag is perhaps, the heaviest at Mr. Jagjivan Ram's residence, where five men have been specially pressed into service to deal with it. Apart from the horde of letters from home and abroad and telegrams and letters proclaiming—"thousands joining you", Babuji receives, like the two party offices, innumerable number of letters from those who profess to be expert astrologers.

MATRIMONIAL LETTER

Correct the following letter:

March 17, 1987

Dear Sar,

Reference your addvertizemant in the matremuneal colams of the Handasthan Timmes, eye give bellow the pertiaklars of the gerl in quistchen:

Age :   2 and 21 years
Data of berth: 1965 May 10

Hite :　　　cms 1.58
Comeplection:　　Fare
Feechur:　　Shorp and attraktive
Heelth:　　Goud. Sleem.

Shee deed her Seneer Kambrige (ISC) from Frunk entony Public Skool and latter gradjuated with Honoors in Hestary from Ledi Seehri Ram Kollege, New Delhi. Shee has allso sukessfuly kompleted a one-year kourse of Seenir Sekretarial Praktice from new Delhi poly teknik far Memen. See iz throughly akkompliced intillegint and fully conversent with household effares.

Shee has won younger brather who has apeered far Sennior Kambrije (ISC) in the kurrant term.

Boothe perants or will ejucated and kultchered. One 1/2 and 2 story hoose at the abave adress. Father is warking in a phoren imbacy in new Dilli; manthly in come over Rss fsix 000. On car. The femily ess vary soshial, respektable and wall connexted.

If thee obave partikulars soot you, kendly let me have semilaar detales of the yoang man and his family. Kend reegarlz.

Correct version

March 14, 1987

Dear Sir,

Reference your advertisement in the matrimonial columns of the Hindustan Times, I give below the particulars of the girl in question:

Age: $21\frac{1}{2}$ years

Date of birth: 18 May 1965

Height: 158 cms

Complexion: Fair

Features: Sharp and attractive

Health: Good Slim

She did her Senior Cambridge (ISC) from Frank Anthony Public School and later graduated with Honours in History from Lady Shri Ram College, New Delhi. She has also successfully completed a one-year Course of Senior Secretarial Practice from the New Delhi Polytechnic for Women. She is thoroughly accomplished, intelligent and fully conversant with household affairs.

She has one younger brother who has appeared for Senior Cambridge (ISC) in the current term.

Both parents are well educated and cultured. Own $2\frac{1}{2}$ storey house at the above address. Father is working in a foreign Embassy in New Delhi; monthly income over Rs. 25,000. Own car. The family is very social, respectable and well connected.

If the above particulars suit you, kindly let me have similar details of the young man and his family.

Kind regards.

30

LITTLE LETTER LAPSES

There are some little omissions and commissions in letter-writing which need your special attention and care.

1. Mr. Ram Singh Esq.   ☒
    Mr. Ram Singh.
    Ram Singh Esq.   ☑

2. Date : April 4, 1997   ☒
    Dated April 4, 1997   ☑

3. April, 4th, 1997   ☒
    4th April, 1997   ☑

4. 4 April, 1997   ☒
    April 4, 1997   ☑

5. Dear Madame.   ☒
    Dear Mesdames.   ☑

6. Sirs and Madams.   ☒

Gentlemen and Ladies. ☑

7. With reference your advertisement in the
   Hindustan Times dated...... ☒

   With reference to your advertisement in
   the Hindustan Times dated....... ☑

8. Thank for your letter. ☒
   Thanks for your letter. ☑

9. Thanks for your letter of 19th proximo. ☒
   Thanks for your letter of 19th ultimo. ☑

10. I will come to you on 25th ultimo. ☒
    I will come to you on 25th proximo. ☑

11. I beg to apply for post of a clerk. ☒
    I beg to apply for the post of a clerk. ☑

12. Per reference your above letter..... ☒
    Per reference to your letter above.... ☑

13. Please accept my heartiest sympathies on
    the death of your mother. ☒

    Please accept my heart-felt sympathies on
    the death of your mother. ☑

14. I offer you my heart-felt congratulations
    on your marriage. ☒

    I offer you my heartiest congratulations
    on your marriage. ☑

15. Your sincerely. ☒
    Yours sincerely. ☑

16. Yours affectionate son. ☒
    Your affectionate son. ☑

17. Your most obediently. ☒
    Yours most obediently. ☑

18. Anticipate an early reply ☒
    Anticipating an early reply. ☑

19. Glad received your letter dated.... ☒
    Glad to receive your letter dated.... ☑

20. Cordially your. ☒
    Cordially yours. ☑

21. Your sincerely friend. ☒
    Yours sincerely.
    Your sincere friend. ☑

22. Please reply quickly. ☒
    Please reply soon. ☑

23. Please reply soon as possible. ☒
    Please reply as soon as possible. ☑

24. Please reply earlier. ☒
    Please reply at your earliest. ☑

25. Do me the favour to send Rs.100. ☒
    Do me the favour of sending Rs.100. ☑

26. Reply without failing. ☒
    Reply without fail. ☑

27. Hope your are hail and hearty. ☒
    Hope you are hale and hearty. ☑

28. Pay my complements to your father. ☒
    Pay my compliments to your father. ☑

29. Give my respect to your mother. ☒
    Pay my respects to your mother. ☑

30. Give my respects to children. ☒
    Give my love to children. ☑

31. Everybody is quite at home. ☒
    Everybody is quite well at home. ☑

32. When you are coming? ☒
    When are you coming? ☑

33. Omissions and commissions accepted. ☒
    Omissions and commissions excepted. ☑

34. Give my message to your friend. ☒
    Convey my message to your friend. ☑

35. Please send receipt. ☒

Please acknowledge receipt. ☑

36. Send US $ 100 on Money Order. ☒
    Send US $ 100 by Money Order. ☑

37. I am anxious awaiting for your reply. ☒
    I am anxiously waiting for your reply.
    I am anxiously awaiting your reply. ☑

Letter written in wrong manner:

Dear Sire

Do you give reference to raw yuth upon aged, maturety and experience. If Yes, the aplikatoshun is of no youz too you. Weather No, you will not find a batter applikant to art and indostree then meself.

I have a wast experience in all branches and departments of art wheech should stand handy to meet your requirements.

I is age man but very youthful spirit with experience and understanding of ort in wheech I have sunk and invited a bitter part off my life.

I am fully traned and experimented in desining magazines, titles. I have kumprehincive noleg about labaouts, littering, printing, block-making, fotografy, sinma slides, poster desining, show-kards, press kartuns, etc.

Thinking you for a early intervue and a praktikal test if you or inklind to emplay only the most competant kandidat for the job advertized by you. Your faithful.

Right manner:

Dear Sir,

Do you give preference to raw youth over age, maturity and experience? If YES, the application is of no use to you. If NO, you will not find a better applicant to art and industry than myself.

I have a vast experience in all branches and departments of art which should stand handy to meet your requirements.

I am an aged man but very youthful in spirit with experience and understanding of art in which I have sunk and invested a better part of my life.

I am fully trained and experienced in designing magazine titles. I have comprehensive knowledge about layouts, lettering, printing, block making, photography, cinema slides, poster designing, show-cards, press cartoons, etc.

Thanking you for an early interview and a practical test if your are inclined to employ only the most competent candidate for the job advertised by you.

Yours faithfully,

ABC

31

PICK-ME-UP PAIRS

There are certain words which are likely to be confused and one is apt to use the wrong word instead of the right one.

1. What is the fair from Delhi to Mumbai? ☒
    What is the fare from Delhi to Mumbai? ☑

2. The girl is very fare. ☒
    The girl is very fair. ☑

3. There is a fare in the village. ☒
    There is a fair in the village. ☑

4. She preys in the temple. ☒
   She prays in the temple. ☑

5. The hunter prays a tiger. ☒
   The hunter preys on a tiger. ☑

6. What are the affects of war? ☒
   What are the effects of war? ☑

7. How does this news effect you? ☒
   How does this news affect you? ☑

8. I do not sea any fetcher here. ☒
   I do not see any future here. ☑

9. The sailor has gone to see. ☒
   The sailor has gone to the sea. ☑

10. The lion ceased a lamb. ☒
    The lion seized a lamb. ☑

11. The Government has seized to exist. ☒
    The Government has ceased to exist. ☑

12. He stood bale for me. ☒
    He stood bail for me. ☑

13. This is a bail of cotton. ☒
    This is a bale of cotton. ☑

14. This is a window pain. ☒
    This is a window pane. ☑

15. I have pane in my ear. ☑
    I have pain in my ear. ☑

16. There is no man hear. ☒
    There is no man here. ☑

17. I have met there mother. ☒
    I have met their mother. ☑

18. I find a rat hear. ☒
    I find a rat here. ☑

19. I cannot here you. ☒
    I cannot hear you. ☑

20. I went there to. ☒
    I went there too. ☑

21. I want too meet you. ☒
    I want to meet you. ☑

22. I do not eat meet. ☒
    I do not eat meat. ☑

23. I want to meat you. ☒
    I want to meet you. ☑

24. This is a strait road. ☒
    This is a straight road. ☑

25. My life is hard and straight. ☒
    My life is hard and strait. ☑

26. Give me a peace of paper. ☒
    Give me a piece of paper. ☑

27. I do not find any piece here. ☒
    I do not find any peace here. ☑

28. The child wants a dear. ☒
    The child wants a deer. ☑

29. This girl is very deer. ☒
    This girl is very dear. ☑

30. We lived in the rain of Indira. ☒
    We lived in the reign of Indira. ☑

31. Rein falls in summer. ☒
    Rain falls in summer. ☑

32. The rain of the horse is broken. ☒
    The rein of the horse is broken. ☑

33. It is reigning night and day. ☒
    It is raining night and day. ☑

34. Things are becoming vary deer. ☑
    Things are becoming very dear. ☑

35. I cot a bird. ☒
    I caught a bird. ☑

36. I lie in a caught. ☒
    I lie in a cot. ☑

37. We have a caught by the see. ☒
    We have a cot by the sea. ☑

38. Women perform many rights. ☒
    Women perform many rites. ☑

39. It is not rite that you should go. ☒
    It is not right that you should go. ☑

40. The old lady has no site now. ☒
    The old lady has no sight now. ☑

41. I went to the sight of the house. ☒
    I went to the site of the house. ☑

42. I reed a newspaper. ☒
    I read a newspaper. ☑

43. The pen is made of read. ☒
    The pen is made of reed. ☑

44. She is a goad girl. ☒
    She is a good girl. ☑

45. Praise is good to success. ☒

Praise is a goad to success. ☑

46. I do not no your name. ☒

I do not know your name. ☑

47. He cannot say know to you. ☒

He cannot say 'no' to you. ☑

48. She has gone to Roam. ☒

She has gone to Rome. ☑

49. Why are you roming here? ☒

Why are you roaming here? ☑

50. This is knot good for you. ☒

This is not good for you. ☑

51. She tied a not. ☒

She tied a knot. ☑

52. This book is for sail. ☒

This book is for sale. ☑

53. The ship is saling on the see. ☒

The ship is sailing on the sea. ☑

32

PRINTER'S DEVIL

You cannot run away from the Printer's Devil. There is hardly any book ever printed in the world which is free from mistakes. Eyes often jump and the proof-reader is likely to pass over a wrong word, however, conscientious he may be. Sometimes, compositors and proof-readers make the right words wrong through lack of knowledge.

1. Subba Rao was apposition choice. ☒
   Subba Rao was opposition's choice. ☑

2. Congress was outnumbered in Lok Sabha. ☒
   Congress was outmanoeuvred in Lok Sabha. ☑

3. The names are not agried upon. ☒
   The names are not agreed upon. ☑

4. I purpose your name. ☒
   I propose your name. ☑

5. The Congress will except this idea. ☒
   The Congress will accept this idea. ☑

6. They submitted their manes. ☒
   The submitted their names. ☑

7. A meating was held. ☒
   A meeting was held. ☑

8. The news are wrong. ☒
   The news is wrong. ☑

9. The contest was envitable. ☒
   The contest was inevitable. ☑

10. The Prime Minister was an abel lady. ☒
    The Prime Minister was an able lady. ☑

11. There were informale talks. ☒
    There were informal talks. ☑

12. M.P.'s move for amety. ☒
    M.P.'s move for amity. ☑

13. Fresh controversey. ☒
    Fresh controversy. ☑

14. Delhi wheather. ☒
    Delhi weather. ☑

15. Premair of India. ☒
    Premier of India. ☑

16. Wot a life. ☒
    What a life! ☑

17. US gives loans to boast Indian farming. ☒
    US gives loan to boost Indian farming. ☑

18. The meating was defered. ☒
    The meeting was deferred. ☑

19. Accarding to police. ☒
    According to police. ☑

20. MP's want penals. ☒
    MP's want panels. ☑

21. Seven billed in clash. ☒
    Seven killed in clash. ☑

22. There was a village fued. ☒
    There was a village feud. ☑

23. World Bank ade. ☒
    World Bank aid. ☑

24. Delgations. ☒
    Delegations. ☑

25. State Assembiles. ☒
    State Assemblies. ☑

26. To many people. ☒
    Too many people. ☑

27. The meeting is of. ☒
    The meeting is off. ☑

28. Four more college. ☒
    Four more colleges. ☑

29. Bang shatters widow-pains. ☒
    Bang shatters window panes. ☑

30. There was colurful fashan prade. ☒
    There was a colourful fashion parade. ☑

31. Mere suger for Delhi. ☒
    More sugar for Delhi. ☑

32. His request was refusde. ☒
    His request was refused. ☑

33. Today Telivesion. ☒
    Today's Television. ☑

33

SOLVED EXERCISES

The following passages are given by way of exercise to the reader so that he can use his intellect to spot out the mistakes. Every passage is accompanied with a corrected passage.

I

SCHOOL FOR MINISTERS

Correct this passage:

New Delhi, March 28:

(UNI)—Ministers should be sent too a training camp to lern what to anser queschuns in Parliament, Mr. Raj Narain (SSP) suggests in the Rjya Sabha yesterday.

Chairwoman Zakir Hussain you will not be in the training camp.

Mr. Raj Narain I shall be a teacher there.

These exchanges folloed a rekwest by Mr. Babubhai Chinai (Congress) that the Chairman should fix a tyme limit for every question in consultion with the leeders of the vareous groups. Mr. Chiani sad of lait only thry of fore kweshens were delt with every day.

Mr. C. Ramchandran suppored Mr. Chinai's sugestion he said full dress debates was going on inn the house a kweschen hower.

A opposition member said whether ministers come well prepaired they were be able to deel with mour kweschens kwickly Often, kweschens repeet because Miinister id not give say this factory reeply.

The Chairman sad he was look in the metre and sea what is dun.

Corrected Passage:

New Delhi, March 28 (UNI)—Ministers should be sent to a training camp to learn how to answer questions in Parliament, Mr. Raj Narain (SSP) suggested in the Rajya Sabha today.

Chairman Zakir Hussain : "You will not be in the training camp".

Mr. Raj Narain: "I shall be a teacher there".

These exchanges followed a request by Mr. Babubhai Chinai (Cong.) that the Chairman should fix a time limit for each question in consultation with leaders of the various groups. Mr. Chinai said of late only three or four questions were dealt with each day.

Mr. G. Ramchandran supported Mr. Chinai's suggestion. He said "full-dress debates" were going on in the House at question hour.

An opposition member said if Ministers came well prepared, they would be able to deal with more questions quickly. Often, questions were repeated because Ministers did not give satisfactory replies.

The Chairman said that he would look into the matter and see what could be done.

II
TRAINING FOR PARLIAMENT

Correct the following passage:

Mr. Raj Narain is at constructive beast in suggesting a training kamp to insruct ministers in the hart of ansering parliament kweschens the only falt we can find is that perhapes the purposal is to restrictive. Mr. Narain cannot be blamed he is respanding to a partikular sichuashun having had tyme to thenk it our he was soorly bee first to reelize that the oposition must naught be dinied the benefits of such an instchushun and sum may argu the press to culd do with instruksun.

Nathing has less then a universty can do ful justie to parliamentry rekuirments but in vue of the kurent need to cut expendichur by the bone priorty mite be given to a few selected subjekts an outsider for instanc ocasionally got the impershun that a compulary coarseentiled how a disagre with the government without disagreing with each other mite help oposition groups.

selksoun of sootable instrktors is present ho problms it is naught far out sider to make detailed suggestions and the ability of congress and opposeetion leeders to kumpose ag agried leasr, when st is in the puqliek inteerest nead not be douted. Sum selkshunr aro self-evidant if he can posibily find thee time mr. narain himself was be persuad. ed to heed the department of parliamentary decooram.

Corrected Passage:

Mr. Raj Narain is at his constructive best in suggesting a training camp to instruct Ministers in the art of answering parliamentary questions. The only fault we can find is that perhaps the proposal is too restrictive. Mr. Narain cannot be blamed: he was responding to a particular situation. Having had time to think it over, he will surely be the first to realize that the Opposition must not be denied the benefits of such an institution. And, some may argue, the Press too could do with instruction.

Nothing less than a University would do full justice to parliamentary requirements. But in view of the current need to cut expenditure to the bone, priority might be given to a few selected subjects. An outsider, for instance, occasionally gets the impression that a compulsory course entitled "How to disagree with the Government without disagreeing with each other" might help Opposition groups.

Selection of suitable instructors should present no problems. It is not for outsiders to make detailed suggestion; and the ability of Congress and Opposition leaders to compose an agreed list, when it is in the public interest, need not be doubted. Some selections are self-evident. If he can possibly find the time, Mr. Narain himself should be persuaded to head the Department of Parliamentary Decorum.

III
TOO HOT TO HOLD

Correct the following passage:

Berne, April 1 (AP) Sevtlana Stalina is still sumwhere in switzerland, but diplomatik sorses say india may turn out to bee her permanent heavan.

The sorses say a return to russia is rooled out for reeligious and politikal reezons and that the united states and switzerland are not eeger for another prickly diplomatik issoo.

Swiz and foreign diplomats say a praces of alimination makes India the most likely sanchur for the 42 year-old svetlana.

They site repart fram India that she has bakum a hindu and is not likely to want to return to her hoamland where religion is discourjed. A soviet sorse in switzerland also said it would be politikally complikated for her to return hoam.

Switzerland almost sertainly well naught bekom her adapted cuntree the swiss government allready feals that it has taken on a jab to hot too handel.

The swiz say protekting stalins datter who's life had been threatened akordin to the Indian reports will be to much furthermour svetlana kud hardli feal sekure in such an atmosfere.

Svetlana arived in New Delhi in janvery with the ashes of brajesh sing an Indian she lived with in moscow this might be a farther motivashum for her to seattle their.

Corrected Passage:

Berne, April 1 (AP)—Svetlana Stalina is still somewhere in Switzerland, but diplomatic sources say India may turn out to be her permanent heaven.

The sources say a return to Russia is ruled out for religious and political reasons and that the United States and Switzerland are not eager for another prickly diplomatic issue.

Swiss and foreign diplomats say a process of elimination makes India the most likely sanctuary for the 42-year-old Svetlana.

They cite reports from India that she has become a Hindu and is not likely to want to return to her homeland where religion is discouraged. A Soviet source in Switzerland also said it would be "politically complicated" for her to return home.

Switzerland, almost certainly, will not become her adopted country. The Swiss Government already feels that it has taken on a job too hot to handle.

The Swiss say protecting Stalin's daughter—whose life has been threatened according to Indian reports—will be too much. Furthermore, Svetlana could hardly feel secure in such an atmosphere.

Svetlana arrived in New Delhi in January with the ashes of Brijesh Singh, an Indian she lived with, in Moscow. This might be a further motivation for her to settle there.

IV
POPE CRITICIZES CAPITALISM

Correct the following passage:

Vatican, march 28 (reuter)—pope paul VI tomorrow critisized sertain as pekts of the kapitalist cistum as he maid a strong plee for rich nashuns to help underdevluped kuntries.

The pope said it is unforchunate that a cistum has been construkted which kunsiders prophet as the kiy motive for economic pragress, kumpetition as the supreme low of economics and private onership as meens of produkshun a absolute rite that had no soshall obligashun.

In his papal encyklical a letter to the words 550 milleen roman catholiks the pontiff attacked the rich fir keeping wat they do not nead landoners for missusing there wast properties and men who mony from a cuntri and transfered it abroad.

The spurfloos weelth off the reach kuntrees must bee plaed at the serbice of pour nashums he say.

The pope repeated a kall he maid in Mumbai in 1964 for world fund takn fram arms expendichur to be used to releeve mens mizery.

Corrected Passage:

Vatican, March 29 (Reuter)—Pope Paul VI yesterday criticized certain aspects of the capitalist system as he made a strong plea for rich nations to help under-developed countries.

The Pope said it was unfortunate that a system had been constructed which considered profit as the key motive for economic progress, competition as the supreme law of economics and private ownership, as means of production, an absolute right that had no social obligation.

In his papal encyclical—a letter to the world's 550 million Roman Catholics—the Pontiff attacked the rich for keeping what they did not need, landowners for misusing their vast properties and men who drained money from a country and transferred it abroad.

The superfluous wealth of rich countries must be placed at the service of poor nations, he said.

The Pope repeated a call he made in Mumbai, in 1964, for a world fund taken from arms expenditure to be used to relieve man's misery.

V

MORE SUGAR FOR DELHI

Correct the following passage:

New delhi, april 1, a addishunal 5000 quintals of sooger have been aloted too the delli administrashun to unable it too tide our the akute sooger shortage in the seety.

It's moonthli kota has been increesed from the preasent 60,000 kuintals to 65,000 kwintals. Inishally this increase will be ephactive for thry months.

The decision to increase the sooger kota was taken too day on a meating of representtivs of the dilli administrashun with unian fod minister Jagjivan Ram the deputashun comrized it Governur Jha, Cheef exekutive counsellor V.K. Malhotra and executive counsellor Ramlal verma.

Weeth the alokation of mour sooger their well bee know cute inn the weakly sooger rashun of 150 grams the blak kunsumers well hooever kontinue to get reodosed kotas.

The dilli administration has decided to fix sooger kotas far the permit hoolders on a new bacis.

The administrashum has approoched the U.P. Government too show the impost of Khandsari in the kapital on a permit bacis.

Corrected Passage:

New Delhi, April 1—An additional 5,000 quintals of sugar has been allotted to the Delhi Administration to enable it to tide over the acute sugar shortage in the city.

Its monthly quota has been increased from the present 60,000 quintals to 65,000 quintals. Initially this increase will be effective for three months.

The decision to increase the sugar quota was taken today at a meeting of representatives of Delhi Administration with Union Food Minister, Jagjivan Ram. The deputation comprised Lt. Governor Jha, Chief Executive Councillor, V.K. Malhotra and Executive Councillor, Ramlal Verma.

With the allocation of more sugar, there will be no cut in the weekly sugar ration of 150 grams. The bulk consumers will, however, continue to get reduced quotas.

The Delhi Administration has decided to fix the sugar quotas for the permit holders on a new basis.

The Administration has approached the U.P. Government to allow the import of khandsari in the capital on a permit basis.

34

UNSOLVED EXERCISES

I

THE POT AND THE KETTLE

Radio Moscow new indignently reports that Chinese diplomats stashoned in Africa, have been ordered to set up militant African Red Guard units. This charge will prabably stick because of Mr. Chou En-lai's publik declaration, during his 1965 visit to Tanzaia, that Africa was ripe for revolution. Chinese involvement in the prospekt had been established earlier when the Chinese Ambassador in Burundi was ordered out of the kuntree, following the asasination of the country's Premier. After the 1965 coups in Dahomey and in the Central African Republic the Chinese Embassies their were also closed. After President Nkrumah's downfall the Chinese were ordered out of Ghana as well.

But even though Peking may be set on exporting its cultural revolution to Africa, what is to be said for Russia's own intervention in African affairs?

The Soviet polisee of arming Algeria against Morocco and Somalia against Ethopia may be more sofistikated but does not appear to be less responsible for creating instability in Afrcia than Peking's kall for direct akshun.

II

KIDNAPPING GIRLS IN DELHI

New Delhi, March 30—About 100 cases of kidnaping of girls or being reopened by the Delhi police.

This girls have been missing for periods ranging from too months to two years.

The police had earlier closed the cases far want of clues. They have now being reopend in the lite of yesterday's statement by the Union Home Minister.

The police has recovered 400 girls reported, missing during the last two years.

According to police officials, there is nothing usual about reports of 500 girls missing in two years in view of the present economic and social background.

The officials regreted that, whil most parents were ken to see their girls back, they wear reluctant to help the police in taking the kidnappers to task. "That is why a large number of solved kidnapping cases fail in the courts", they said.

Besides, the girls about 2,000 children under 12 years of age, were reported missing during the past one year. About 98 per cent of them have been restored to their parents.

Chavan's asurence:

The Delhi police officials investigating the alleged kidnaping of Miss Kamla Vohra have been instrukte to chek affidavits and other declarations filled in the courts of magistrates in Delhi, U.P., Punjab, Rajasthan and Himachal Prades after March 7, the day the Delhi girls disappeard.

The polic parties which had gon to Bhopal, Moradabad and other U.P. tons today returnd withoot an success. Some people who were believed to have scene Miss Vohra in Moradabad on March 9 were being questioned.

Mr. B.L. Vohra, father of the girl, and members of his family today met Home Minister Chavan and requested him to transfer the investigation of the case to some other agency. Mr. Chavan is said to have assured him that every efort would be maid to trase the girl.

According to a late night report another police party left for agra this evening following infarmashun about the presence of Miss Vohra there.

III

DEBATE ON PRESIDENT'S ADDRESS

New Delhi April 3—The resumed Lok Sabha debait today on the President's Address was enlivened by Dr. Karni Singh's forthrite speech in which he asked the opposition groups to unite and behave decently as they may be asked to form a government at the Centre in the near future.

With U.P. gon and two-third of India "out of the clutches of the Congress", in another six month the oposition parties may find themselves on the Treasury bench. They must give up their political squables and become a homogenous unit, he said.

Dr. karni Singh who was cheered by section of the House prefacd his remark by saying that he stod for oposition solidarity but he was aginst "character asassination" indulged in by some members. If the privat lives of members of Parliament, taken collectively, wer open for inspection to a reserch student, we will have a best seller. Non of us are Buddhas. We all hav human failing. Let thos who live in glas houses not thro stone at others".

In an obvious refrence to allegations that the Prime Minister had received costly gifts, he said responsible citizens in this country should not encourage this type of blackmale." The Government ought to be, put on the mut if there was something wrong but 'let us not have political vendettas or blackmale."

Un-Indian

Refering to the us of the word "Badmashi" during the question tim taday by Mr. Madhu Limaye, Dr. Karni Singh qoted a dictionry in support of his contention that the world should not have been used in Parliamentry procedings, although the speaker had

214

held to the contary. Such exprsions were 'un-Indian'. Even if their English equivalents found their way into Hansard the British have their standards, but let us have ours.

Members of Pliament had to hehave with dignity. They could not introduce the "vegetable market" atmosphere into Parliament.

He argued that a non-Congress Government may come into power at the Centre sooner then many people realized. The oposition parties must unite : they could even put up a pretty lady as Prime Minister or have a 'de jure' Depty Prime Minister. If the non Congress Government did nothing about the question of povrty, unemployment and hunger they would share the same fate as the Congress.

Another highliht of today's debate was a speech by Mr. C.C. Desai (Swa) who complained that the prime Minister was further thinking of expanding the already expanded kitchen Cabinet' to include two State Ministers and 17 Parliamentary Secrtaries regardless of the cost of the Exchequer.

Mr. R.K. Amin (Swa) said economic advance was not possible without agricultural revolution. He wanted agricultural graduates to be drafted for agricultural work zonal barries to be removed and remunerative pricis for formers fixed.

Mrs. Mohindra Kaur and Mrs. Sushila Rohtagi, both Congress, wanted more efforts to be put into polularzing family planning. Mrs. Kaur even wanted abortion to be legalized to keep down birth rate.

The debate, well continue tomorrow and the Prime Minister will reply on Wednesday. From tomorrw, the House will sit up to 7 p.m. daily to be able to dispose of the Constitution (21 Amendment) Bill and the Finance Bill, among other things.

IV

MINNY FASHION

New Delhi, march 27—If the "mini" ever landed in space, it still manage to look a down to earth garment to move about, practical, earthly.

And Pierre Cardin, the fashion desiner from Paris who showed a part of his collection at Ashoka Hotel, tomorrow, tells you why.

But Cardin and his four models, flon in from Paris have something more than the 'mini' to them. As a packed hall including Prime Minister Indira Gandhi, Dr. Karna Singh and a number of foreign dignitories watched the sho, Cardin unpacked his surprize package on by won.

His models do not move—they just guided non-stop on a snowwhite stage. If Cardin's aim was to catch the eye he certanly succeeded remarkably in that.

The garments shown at today's fashion show were displayed at a recent fashion, parade in Paris. Quite a few of the 150 garments were rather startling The in Paris.

It is in woolens that Cardin is at his best and most imaginative. Milk and chocolate, bright canary yellow 'minis' the sheerest of ple greens, buckled at the hip, with disk hats peached on the top or a space cap with a board brime shading the face—all looked lovely and smart.

And all his garments are a sheer comfort to move in 'Out' is the tight look both for men and women; in are the swirling dreses.

The model with the-butter-would-not-melt-in-her-mouth look-took the palm with white woolen dress with black bordered hem, neckline and cufs. Another, demure in her while and navy-blue, got her share of applause. A Scottish tartan with red, green and black bold squares was a marvel.

Cardin's chiffons for the long summer, evening would be any women's delight. There also is an imposible lotstel collars and cuffs which looked lovely on a long white woolen dres.

It is rather hard to describe the Cardin line increases. But he asents Leshaped sleeveless style in womens clothes and close shoulders, long slits at the coatbacks inn men's dresses.

V

THE UNTOLD STORY

An important point to be remembered is that the civilian power in a demokracy must enjoy a overiding authorety over the armed forces and that the armed forces must keep away from politic. It follow therefore, that in the choice off selecting its advisers in the sphere of defence and making appointments at the top level, a final voice must be with the Civil Authority. Naturally this authority must be exercised in the best interest of the country and wher it is not so exercised, condemnation cannot be to serve. It is here that the untold story is fully told. Note because General Kaul does not wish to but because he knows only end of it General Caul explain what hit qualifications were on the important question is weare there others better sited? The importance of the question lies in the fact that the feeling is entertained that the Defence Minister at the time, in the sure knowledge that Nehru was behind him, was playing a deep hand. If, it was wrongly entertained; it should be so proved. Even before the Chines attack, the record of V.V.K. Menon as High Commissioner U.K. had been highly unsatisfactory. Vast sums of mony, millions in fact had been last in the arms deals alone by this champion, can be that it was culpable neglinence but is it the only one? Coupled with his longheld political and ideological viws his stewrdship off the defence deparment was disasterous.

VI

PARK FOR KINGS

With an elaboratly planed park is bing laid out of a cost of nearly Rs. 34 lakhs to house the statues of British monarches and viceroys removed from the city, five of these statves lie shorn of their magnificence, covered with filth and tattered bits of sackloth in a desorted corner in the exhibition ground ate Mathura Road, Delhi.

Asked where the statues were being kept, a spokesman of the CPWD replied that they "are lying wrapped up and packed in CPWD stores and are bing looked after very well".

The store is only an impromised enclosur covered with tin sheets on four sides. No rof shelfters the statue. They lie flat on the ground. Thorny hushes several feet high surounded encloure.

The statue of Lord Irwin, its nos brokeen, its chisellod features battered, lies covered wih dirty cloth peaces probably put out to dry over it at one stage.

In another cornor is Lord Hardinge, his nose peering out from a torn sack, brick lying ironcally havy on his heart. The sand-bags which should have supported the status from below have long since trickled to emptiness and what were once gunny bag converings are nowhere to be scene.

The battered but majestice walls of Purana Quila stand looking down on the strtus and they with thir sunkin eyes carvd out in cold-white marble seem to gaze up in mute wonder.

Rain water infested with dirt and insects fills the hollowed portion of the status.

While this is the fate of the status the authorities' uncaring and oblivous, have resumed work on the 48-acre Cornation Park.

In this park, situated at the end of a long winding road and rubbing shoulders with the dancing green fields of Haryana village, the statues will repose in solitary splendor. Work on the park had to be suspended following a ban on all construction by the Planning Commission a few years ago.

It is a tuff battle that the authorities are fighting there to make the park a suitable place to house the statues of viceroys. The entire land is covered with saline soil on which little vegetation can grow.

It is now proposed to construct a kutcha dam and instal a pump to wash down the saline into a drane being built for the purpose.

The part is to be developed in three phases. During the current phase 150 varieties of bushes and shrubs, mostly those which can thrive on saline soil, will be planted. Casuarina trees which or nurtured on salinity will dot the spots where there is the largest concentration of salt.

Five specially disind pedestals will be built for the statues. As yet a solitary pedestal stand in the vast empriness of the park. The only other structure is the coronation pillar.

The first to be moved in will be the five stachoos of Lord Irwin, Lord Reading, Lord Chelmsford. Lord Hardinge and Lord Willngdon, which or lying in the exhibition grounds the statue of Queen Victoria outside the Town Hall including Chandi Chowk and that of King George V near India Gate.

During the second phase the park will be given a face lifts and roads and pavements constructed. In the last phase a 12-foot wide meendering stream will be laid which will run through the entire park and wash away any remaining salinity. On the slopes now scarred with black burnt out marks will trail bougainvillageas in a riot of colour.

VII

SILVER SCREEN GIRL

Mangala, a filmstruck girl in her teens dreaming of a life of glamour, deserted her parents and with a trunk full of cloths and some money pilfered from her parents, arrived at Hyderabad. A night's lonely travel in the crowded railway compartment had already dissipated much of her bravado and in the ensuing confusion she got down at Secunderabad Station instead of at Kachiguda, where she expected to seek shelter with the family of a aquaintance. But fait willed otherwise for poor Mangala.

Having got down in an unknown place, the lonely girl was bewildered. Not having much experience in travelling and dealing with people, she was at a loss to know what next stop she should take and where to spend the night.

Natrajan's Offier

Natarajan, a waiter in the Railway, Restaurant, an old hand of the underworld seeing a loney young girl standing on the platform approached Mangala and showed parental solicitude and took her in the waiting room above. In no time, the girl was the receipient of the stayers of many hangers on and was soon provided with tiffin and hot tea by the waiter. Being modest, Mangala at first refused the volunatrily offered refreshments but under the soft speaking Natrajan's insistance, she partook the offering.

Asked to take rest alone with other women in the waiting room, the girl lost her fear and thanked Natarajan for his kindness.

After Midnight

But how can the young girl see the wolf under the sheep's clothing. At Two O'clock in the night, Natarajan came slinking back to the waiting room along with the ticket collector who asked Mangala to show her ticket.

A more experienced girl than Mangala could have sensed that it was mare bye play by the two scoundrals and have appealed to other women in the waiting room, but natarajan was ready with an offer of alternate accommodation in the nearby Dharmshala. Poor unsuspecting Mangala accompanied the rascal to a nearby bungalow to be met with an old fogey of woman who offered her cordial welcome and showed much concern over the difficulties of a new young girl in a big city.

Reassured by the kind words and solicitude shown by the two sharks, the girl occupied a room allotted to her.

In a Different Part of Bungalow

Next day, Natarajan boosted of his friendship with many film producers and directors assured his best efforts to get Mangala engagement. Both moved in a taxi for some time and the night found the girl again in a different part of the bunglow 8 O'clock and a fat belied man was introduced to Mangala as a famous producer. After some drinks which they said was a must to every up and coming film artist Mangala was seduced by the so-called producer followed by Natrajan who also wanted his share of flesh.

Poor mangala

Being thus cornered and with no avenue of escape poor Mangala satisfied the lust of many and one day seeing the coast clear bolted away from the house of illrepute.

Having last her virtue and with no face to go back to her parents she took the easy wayout by doucing her cloth with keorsene oil and setting herself on fire.

Thus the life of an innocent girl who new very little of life and who aspired to win and easy path to stardum was smashed to smitherns and ended in a grusome tragedy.

This should be a warning to many a wayward young girl who jest because she is a little handsome, tries to imitate glamour girls and becomes a pray of vultures who are always on the lookout of such inncent but sophisticated damsells.

VIII

SEARCH FOR A STYLE

Like many others, the Jan Sangh President has fallen into the error or imagining that the architectural style used in India for tombs, temples and masques is equally suitable for functional buildings. Irritated by what he described as box-like structures built to house Government officers, Mr. Nehru at one time asked for Indian architecture. This was not a little surprising because the same Mr. Nehru defendedly Corbusier's Chandigarh against all criticism. In any case as a result of his desire for the Indian touch we have the Supreme Court building in imitation of Lutyensis hybrid style and Manak Bhavan with its slender colums and unshaply conturs as a hotch-potch of the so-called Indian stiles.

What is wrong with over new public buildings is not that they or not Indian enough, but that they have been designed by unimaginative architects with no mour than academic modern training. In more recent years some of our official architects have been applying there minds to the problem and have not been ignoring the need to inves buildings with an Indian character without sacrifising that principals of functionalism. A case in point is the design for the Indian pavilion in Montreal which based on Jantar Manter in New Delhi.

Since Chandigarh was built architects preparing blue-prints for both for both public and privite buildings have been letting themselves go. In some of the Capital's residentail colonies we have a most unattractive mixture of style. Crazy ideas have been executed in steel and concrete without inhibition. As for public buildings, most of them are not better, but there is evidence to suggest that an effort is definitely being made to evolve a modern Indian style. The healthy trend can lead to something worthwhile only if the disigns and the discussionon them are left to architects and those with the social and aesthetic philosophy of architecture. Sloganizing by politicians can hardly help to developed a style of our own.

IX

MAN KNIFED TO DEATH

By a Staff Correspondent

New Delhi April 1—A 25-year old man was dun to death and another injured in knife attacks on the busy Pusa Road this afternoon.

The alleged assailant, Salamuddin, a junk seller of Suiwalan, ran way from the scene brandishing a bloodstained knife as hundreds of people stood helpless on the road. But he was ourpowered a short distance away. He threw away the knife which had not been recovered till late this evening.

About 1-20 p.m., Salamuddin and Ajit, the victim, came together in a scooter from Jama Masjid to a tea stall on Pusa Raod. They reportedly asked Rajender Pal, the stall holder, for some soda. they also demanded Rs. 20 from him, but he refused.

The two men continued to sit there for some time. Later Ajit asked Salamuddin to pay him Rs. 400 which he owed him. This led to hot words. Rajender Pal asked them to leave the place but they refused to do so.

Salamuddin then wiped out of a knife and attacked Ajit who died on the spot.

Rajender Pal chased the assailant but was attacked with the knife and fell down. Both the victims lay in a pool of blood for nearly half an hour before the police reached the scene.

X

A GOOD GOVERNMENT

Sir,

The roolers would best promote the improvement off the nation by strictly confining themselves to their own lucrative course, commodities their own fare prices, Industries and Intelligence their nature reward. Idleness and fooly their natural punishment. They must help sincerly in maintainence of piece by defending property and reducing the price of law, by observing strict economic in all departments government. If the roolers do as stated about, the people would do the rest.

It is, therefore, necessary that all sorts of controls and restrictions on movements be dun away with. Food zonez must be removed completely, and there should be no controls on gold, cement, sugar and other comodities. Neither should there by any control on houses etc. in the whole country.

If these things are done the central government and by state governments, the prices would come down on their levels and their would be piece throughout the country.

Yours etc.

Anoop Sunder Lal

Advocate, Ghaziabad.

XI

TOTAL REVOLUTION

JP's Total Rvolution iz on the march and like the irresitible waves of the Indian Ocean in monsonns it will cross all borders and will effect the selfish politcs of all neighbouring countries—Nepal, Pakistan, Sri Lanka Bangladesh, Burma, Iran, Afghanistan—and invade the Third world, and compete with Cokommunism in very communistic countries, both in China and Russia.

JP's total revolution is none of his own making. It has a fivine origin and has the propulsive urge of Prophet Mohammad Islam and Budha's Nirvana and Jasus Christ's Sermon on the Mount.

This is what JP writes how he was inspired undertake the Total Revolution:

"It was in the last months of 1973 when I was at Paunar, that I felt an inner urge to give a call to youth".

This happened:" After Prabha's departure I had lost interest inlife. Had I not developed a special apitude for public work, I wouldhave retired to the Himalayas. My heart wept within but outwardly I followed the routine of life. My health too was deteriorating. It was in this hour that something unexpected happened which lit no inner self. My health also stated improving and I experienced a new energy and zeal."

Prompted by the necessity of removing the sufferings of women the globe over of which I have some idea through the lives of my widowed grandmother, my respected (late) mother, my worthy spouse and autobiographies and biographies of some of the women of remote yesterday through today, I have decided to become a woman for I feel that in the form and frame of a man I won't be able to do justice in helping relieve the sufferings of the women, the

Half of the World

I want to raom the globe over with the man's fearless and determined mind fitted in the woman's body, in order to have clearer idea of women's problems and discuss with them the ways and means to improve their lot so that the world may have a better tomorrow for it is the woman who bears the man and because the life on globe would come to and end should the woman ceaze to exist but this won't happen if man is removed. Our heritage which declares "Janan: Janam-bhumishcha swargadapi griyasi" (mother and motherland/fatherland are greater than the Heaven) and Ashley Montaggue's Natural Superiority of Woman (a British publication the other particulars of which have slipped off my memory) have forced me to transform the man in me to a woman.

The women the globe over (and the men who like this idea) are requested to provide me (a) medical literature for conversion of a man into a woman, (b) women's problems and suggestions for their removal, and (c) money to the tune of as little as they can afford through as much as they desire. Indian and non-Indians abroad are requested to send money through their embassies in India or through Indian Embasies stationed in their countries, under advice (intimation) to me.

The money will presently be used for the following purposes, which may go on multplying in future according to the suggestions and criticism of women:

(a) My conversion from man into a woman.

(b) Setting up of a (new) Research Institute for Study and Removal of female problems. For this purpose a programme is to be framed and suggestions in details and suggestive programme are most cordially invited from women in Hindi, Urudu, English (one of these) or in any other language. I have a little knowledge of Sanskrit, Persian and Punjabi languages, also.

2. In addition to the above I hereby dedicate every limb of my body (eyes, ears, nose and everything) for use for the benefit of the physically handicapped persons, particularly for children and women, and research.

For this humble service, I seek the blessings of all the women the globe over who are older than me, good wishes of women of my age, and prayers by younger women.

I was born on the 5th December 1930 at village and Post office Nia shahar, Tehsil Kharar, District Ropar (then District Ambala), Punjab, India and my date of birth was wrongly recorded as 25th November 1931 much before I could know of the mistake.

XII

THE THEME IS ROMANCE

The theme of romance is modernism. The theme of modernism is romance. Unless there is a touch of romance in you, your life is not nice—and without spice! Romance is a superior theme for filmdom than crime or viole rape, pick-pocketing or thuggery. Infact, love is the only subject that all makes your life wrath living.

Consequently, we congratulete M/s Mahajan Film International (30, Meadowe Street, Mumbai-1) for their farthcoming production MOOHABBAT.

Mr. Harish Chawla, a graduate of the Film and Television Institute of India has been signed to wield the megaphone, based on his own story. The film is being produced by producer Surinder Mohan under his new banner Magabajab Film International.

The film will have music by Shyamji Ghamshymiji with lyrics by Abbilsh.

Four promising stars will head the cast of the film. Famous lyrist Varma Malik has been signed to pen the songs for the new film MOOHABBAT be produced by Surinder Mahajan and prem Sharma under their new banner. Music Director Sonik Imi will give musical score for the film.

Mohabbat is expected to be a delightful spextacle for the auduence and the critics—a feast for eyes and food for the soul.

35

GOOD ENGLISH VERSUS CORRECT ENGLISH

It is not sufficient to write correct English. It is even more important to write good English. Good English may not be always correct English and correct English may not be always good English.

When you observe all the laws, rules and regulations of correct English, then you find that good English is murdered. In case of Shakespeare, who wrote the finest English, his writing does not stand up to any test of grammatical laws and regulations. He wrote as he felt. One, who writes as he feels, is divinely inspired he cannot subject himself to the tests and trials of grammatical gadgets. Words flow from Shakespeare in a torrent and torrents don't obey laws.

Therefore, while you should strive to write and speak correct English, do not make it the be-all and end-all of your linguistic efforts at self-improvement. On the contrary, self-improvement itself will become a vehicle for the outpour of your soul.

It is as much important to cultivate the habit of creative thinking as of assiduously studying grammar and spellings. Of course, grammar and spellings are important; but you must look to the psychological domains far beyond them. In the following passages, you will find excellent English which may not always measure up to grammatical expectations. Emulate the style, because it is the type of modern good writing. Your target must be good writing and not necessarily correct writing.

THE REASON WHY

So many of us, given the opportunity to leave India, are only too ready to shake the dust of Hindustan from our feet. And yet I, who have had so many opportunities to go away, hand on like a leech.

What is it that keeps me here? Time and again, I have thought of going away. Sometimes life has been a little rough, and I thought: I can make a better living in Canada like my brother; or in New Zealand like my cousins. But I do not feel attracted towards these places; their very prosperity frightens me. Not so long ago I was offered a well-paid job in Singapore; thought about it for weeks; worried myself to distraction; and breathed a sigh of relief only when I had turned it down.

My friends thought I was mad. They still do. Most of them would have jumped at the offer, even if it had meant spending the rest of their lives far from their native land. Many of my friends do go away to

Britain or the USA or the Far East, and never come back, except perhaps to get married, very quickly, before they are off again. If they do not see India again, it rarely bothers them.

But I am terrified at the thought of going away and then being unable to come back. This almost happened to me when, as a boy, I went to England and did not have enough money to get back. For two years I saved like a mad miser (something I've never done before or since) until I had enough for the passage to India.

So what is it that keeps me here? My birth? I take too closely after a Scandinavian grandparent to pass for a typical son of the soil. But India is where I was born and grew up, India is where my father was born and grew up, India is where my grandfather came as a youth and grew to manhood. Surely that entitles me to a place in the Indian sun? Doesn't it?

Then it must be the land. But so many of my fellow-Indians have been born and re-born here dozens of times, and yet they think nothing when leaving the land. They will leave the mountains for the plains, the villages for the cities, the country for another country. And if other lands would be a little more willing to open their doors, there would be no population problem in India. Mass emigration would have solved it!

The land does hold me: but it's more than the land. For India is more than a land. India is an atmosphere. For over thousands of years the races and religions of the world have commingled here and produced that unique, undefinable phenomenon, the Indian: so terrifying in a crowd, so beautiful in himself. And oddly enough, I'm one too. I know that I'm an Indian as the postman or the paanwala or your favourite M.P. Race didn't make me one; religion didn't make me one; but history did. And in the long run, it's history that counts.

INTERPRETING SMILES

Even the most innocuous subject can spark of a debate. Take for example, the statement: all men smile. Besides suffragette protests over women being left out; the habitual disputant may ask: what proof that there never existed men who never smiled? It is difficult to answer. No one has kept detailed biographical accounts with minute-to minute entries of gestures and words of all men born since the missing link was bridged. But enter the counter-disputationist: what proof that there ever was a man who never smiled?

This reminds one of a basic truth: some debates yield on conclusion; nor do they have an end. One might ask: how does it matter whether all men smile or not? The importance is in the smile, particularly in what it indicates. What does Mona Lisa's smile reveal? It is one of those smiles which cannot be read and can signify both approval and disapproval. Some would dismiss all this as pure trivia, the guessing game of idle minds and assert that a smile is a smile, and that is that.

Not so simple. If a smile is to be called a smile and the curtain drawn after that, why should one insist on calling a spade a spade? And, is one speaking here metaphorically or in plain audio-visual terms? In case of the latter, there is no problem in identifying and naming a spade. But problems arise the moment one enters the confusing world of metaphors, which are mixed frequently and without compunction, despite the grammarians severe frowns. Take for example that famous passage where Hamlet wonders "to be or not to be" and whether it was worth taking up "arms against a sea of troubles".

Fortunately, a smile cannot be metaphorical: it is there for all to see. And some smiles are worth a million, literally, like a woman's going with a toothpaste or lipstick ad, or of a man advertising a highly masculine tie. But there are other unpaid smiles which are worth possible more, that of the baby without a tooth, of the child delighted, or mother beholding her just born. One can go on counting instances.

Reverting to the debate—who can resist the temptation? One can perhaps settle with the conclusion that most men and women smile but there are some unsmiling types. This is true. There are men—and perhaps women—who decide to shoulder the world's worries and never open their mouths, except to convey the most spine-chilling prognostications.

These are the oracles of gloom, taken seriously only at disaster time when people fear the worst.

Normally the preference is for cheerful forecasts and pleasing words. For freedom from anguish, worry and fear are part of the quest for freedom and search for truth which, according to M.N. Roy, whose birth anniversary fell on March 21, are the two basic urges behind human progress. As Roy explained in his famous twenty-two thesis, truth is the content of knowledge and the quantum of freedom in any society depends on the level of its enlightenment.

From the world of metaphors we now enter the world of philosophy, which is even more confusing, involving, as it does, the proverbial chase for the black cat in a dark room when the cat does not exist. It is the world of mindboggling speculation on reality or unreality, of the dichotomy or otherwise of mind and matter, of being and non-being. This is not everyone's cup of coffee. But not everyone makes history, and often philosophy is the latter's dynamite. Beginning with the French, every modern revolution has been set off, albeit directly, by a ferment of ideas. But smiles can almost be powerful. If Helen's face could launch thousand ships, what could here smile do?

DIAL 'P' FOR PRESIDENT

By Raj Chatterjee

The concept of a direct appeal by the humblest of citizens to the highest authority in the land is not new to us.

I forget the name of the Mughal Emperor who had a giant bell installed in the palace courtyard. Anyone wanting and audience with the Shahinshah just had to ring the bell, the sound of which must have been like a death-knell to the rapacious daroga, munsiff or other petty official against whom the bell-ringer had grievance.

I am intrigued to see that the idea, in a modified form, has caught on in the U.S., a country normally associated with all sorts of innovations such as inventing chewing gum and stepping on the moon.

The innovator in this case is no less a person than Mr. Jimmy Carter who seems set on doing things that no other President has done in the two hundred years of American Independence.

It may be recalled that during the period between his election last November and his inauguration in January this year, Mr. Carter made several off-beat statements to the Press, such as, confessing his innermost thoughts to reporters and saying that he would carry his own bags into the White House. I don't know if he actually did so in the end.

Mr. Carter was also the first President to walk instead of riding in a heavily guarded limousine on the day he took his oath of office. I can't remember now if it was from the White House to the Capital or *vice versa*.

And unlike any of his predecessors Mr. Carter prefers to be known by his nickname 'Jimmy' which he uses even when putting his signature to Presidential orders and other State documents.

The latest of Mr. Carter's departures from the norm is to make himself available on the telephone to any American citizen who cares to ring up the White House on a special number between the hours of 2 and 4 p.m. I dare say, though, that even Mr. Carter observes the sabbath as a day of rest.

Computer Aid

Of course, nothing is done in the U.S. without the aid of a computer. It is not surprising, therefore, that one of these ubiquitous gadgets monitors each call to make sure that every region in the country gets its due share of these homely 'citizen-to' chats over the wire.

It would interest me greatly to know if when calling up Mr. Carter the oilman from Texas or the farmer from Ohio addresses him as 'Mr. President' or simply 'Hi, Jimmy'.

Be that as it may, Mr. Carter has undertaken to answer all questions put to him except those that are plainly abusive. Nor will he pay heed to questions that are not 'interesting'.

He has not defined what constitutes an 'uninteresting' question. I should imagine, however, that it would relate to very personal matters such as a chronic pain in the caller's left toe or the trouble he is having with his mother-in-law.

Things are—or have been—a little different in our country. You can certainly talk to a senior official of the government but only after stating the exact nature of your business to his P.A.

Once you have disclosed this, there is a pause during which the P.A. consults his boss on the intercom. If the later considers that your business is not important enough to 'interest' him, the P.A. will give you the name, and possibly the telephone number, of a less senior official who, of course, also has a P.A. The entire process is then repeated and you are likely to be directed to an even less senior official.

And so it goes on till you end up by talking to an Under-Secretary or, at best, a Deputy Secretary.

Let us hope that the new Government will make it easier for unimportant persons like you and I to directly approach the official who can make a decision without having consultation with his superiors.